TEACHING A DIVERSE PRIMARY CURRICULUM

T0354206

SAGE was founded in 1965 by Sara Miller McCune to support the dissemination of usable knowledge by publishing innovative and high-quality research and teaching content. Today, we publish over 900 journals, including those of more than 400 learned societies, more than 800 new books per year, and a growing range of library products including archives, data, case studies, reports, and video. SAGE remains majority-owned by our founder, and after Sara's lifetime will become owned by a charitable trust that secures our continued independence.

Los Angeles | London | New Delhi | Singapore | Washington DC

TEACHING A DIVERSE PRIMARY CURRICULUM

EDITED BY
KARIN DOULL

Learning Matters
A SAGE Publishing Company
1 Oliver's Yard
55 City Road
London EC1Y 1SP

SAGE Publications Inc.
2455 Teller Road
Thousand Oaks, California 91320

SAGE Publications India Pvt Ltd
B 1/I 1 Mohan Cooperative Industrial Area
Mathura Road
New Delhi 110 044

SAGE Publications Asia-Pacific Pte Ltd
3 Church Street
#10-04 Samsung Hub
Singapore 049483

Editor: Amy Thornton
Senior project editor: Chris Marke
Project management: TNQ Technologies
Marketing manager: Lorna Patkai
Cover design: Wendy Scott
Typeset by: TNQ Technologies
Printed in the UK

© 2022 Editorial arrangement, Introduction and Chapter 6: Karin Doull

© 2022 Chapter 2: Helen Crawford © 2021 Chapter 3: Susie Townsend © 2021 Chapter 4: Damienne Clarke and Gary Pykitt © 2021 Chapter 5: Moira Brazil © 2021 Chapter 7: Bente Opheim © 2021 Chapter 8: Paul Bracey © 2021 Chapter 9: Anthony Barlow © 2021 Chapter 10: Sarah Adams and Alison Murray © 2021 Chapter 11: Susan Ogier © 2021 Chapter 12: Kerenza Ghosh © 2021 Chapter 13: Lynda Chinaka, Sue McKinney and Sue Miles-Pearson.

First published in 2022

Apart from any fair dealing for the purposes of research, private study, or criticism or review, as permitted under the Copyright, Designs and Patents Act, 1988, this publication may not be reproduced, stored or transmitted in any form, or by any means, without the prior permission in writing of the publisher, or in the case of reprographic reproduction, in accordance with the terms of licences issued by the Copyright Licensing Agency. Enquiries concerning reproduction outside those terms should be sent to the publisher.

Library of Congress Control Number: 2022935444

British Library Cataloguing in Publication Data

A catalogue record for this book is available from the British Library

ISBN 978-1-5297-8135-9
ISBN 978-1-5297-8134-2 (pbk)

CONTENTS

ABOUT THE EDITOR AND CONTRIBUTORS

The Editor

Karin Doull is a Principal Lecturer at the University of Roehampton. She taught in London schools for over 10 years before coming to Roehampton as a primary history specialist. She is a co-author of *Mastering Primary History* (Bloomsbury, 2020) as well as a series of articles and book chapters. While history is her first love, she also remains convinced that challenging and fulfilling learning lies in the carefully constructed interplay of all subjects within the curriculum. She is keen to promote the integral role that the foundation subjects play in engaging children. She has long been interested in celebrating and exploring woman's history. She is a fellow of the Historical Association and a member of their primary committee. She is editor-in-chief for *Primary History Journal*. She has led CPD events for class teachers, mentors and senior leaders through consultancy work. She has been involved in several funded education research projects working with the National Archive and Imperial War Museum. She is the author of a short story of historical fiction, *The Vexation of Lady Dale*.

The Contributors

Sarah Adams: After eight years working at the University of Roehampton as a Senior Lecturer in Primary Physical Education, Sarah emigrated back to Canada where she is currently working within the education system as a teacher. Her research interests include curriculum design, pre-service teachers and their experience with physical education, and factors contributing to learning and engagement. Sarah enjoys leading CPD events, supporting teachers and mentors, and collaborating with stakeholders across the PE sector both in Canada and the United Kingdom.

Anthony Barlow is Principal Lecturer and subject leader for Geography Education at the University of Roehampton. He teaches initial teacher education courses as part of the undergraduate and post-graduate programmes and is Programme Convenor for the BA Primary Education QTS programme. His principal research focus is pupils' understanding of their locality and especially the built environment. Other professional interests include teaching about the oceans and the environmental pollution issue of plastic waste. He has worked on a number of consultancy projects with Channel 4/Grid Club, Rising Stars, the BBC and TTS. He was until recently the Chair of the Early Years and Primary Committee of the Geographical Association and is now a member of the sub-committee responsible for GeogLive CPD session on YouTube. His recent book with Sarah Whitehouse is published by Bloomsbury and is called *Mastering Primary Geography* (2019). He tweets @totalgeography and @EYPPC_GA.

Paul Bracey is a History Education Consultant having recently retired as Senior Lecturer/Curriculum Leader for Primary History Education at the University of Northampton. He has provided workshops with the Historical Association, School History Project (Primary), HTEN and NASBTT. He is an experienced teacher and teacher educator and writer. Paul is a Fellow and Trustee of the Historical Association, a member of the Primary Education Committee and Primary Editorial Board and Chair of Midlands History Forum. He has a BA (Hons) in Economic History, an MA in History, PGCE and PhD in Education. For the latter he examined the significance of an Irish dimension in the English History Curriculum. His research interests and publications relate to teaching diversity and developing a broadly based understanding of the past.

Moira Brazil is Senior Lecturer in the School of Education, University of Roehampton, and has worked across Greater London as a teacher and consultant. She contributes to Initial Teacher Training routes, leads a module on multilingual learners and convenes a regional interest group for the EAL subject association NALDIC (National Association for Language Development in the Curriculum). She also works with the Bell Foundation delivering Continuing Professional Development on multilingual learners with English as an additional language (EAL).

Lynda Chinaka is Senior Lecturer in the School of Education and a Group Tutor on the PGCE Primary Education Programme at the University of Roehampton. She is a Fellow of the Higher Education Academy. Lynda's teaching career spans a period of over 20 years and work in four diverse London Boroughs. She has led the development of computing in schools in various roles as well as Teacher Leader for a local London Authority's School Improvement Service. She is an Associate Facilitator of the National Centre of Computing Education and a member of the grassroots computing community – Computing At schools (CAS). Keenly passionate about access to computing for everyone, Lynda is an advocate of promoting culturally relevant and responsive computing in the classroom.

Damienne Clarke is Senior Lecturer in Primary and Early Years Education at Birmingham City University, specialising in primary history. She is a former primary school teacher and head teacher and was history subject leader in a number of primary schools. Damienne is Co-secretary of the Midlands History Forum and a member of the Historical Association's *Primary History Journal* Editorial Board, regularly contributing to the publication. Damienne and Gary Pykitt have co-presented primary history workshops around teaching LGBT+ inclusive history for the Historical Association.

Helen Crawford is Senior Lecturer in Primary Education at the University of Northampton. She has worked in education for over twenty years as an early years teacher, primary teacher and school leader. Helen is an author of the *Oxford International Primary History* series (Oxford University Press, 2017) and a consultant for BBC Bitesize primary history. She is a member of the Historical Association Primary Committee, member of the editorial board for *Primary History Journal* and an honorary fellow of the Historical Association.

Kerenza Ghosh is Senior Lecturer in English Education at the University of Roehampton in London. She has contributed chapters to academic books about primary education and has co-authored an article about student teachers' use of comics in the primary classroom. Kerenza has presented research papers at conferences in the United Kingdom and Europe, and has a Master's in Critical Approaches to Children's Literature from the University of Cambridge. She has a published chapter entitled *Who's*

Afraid of the Big Bad Wolf: Children's Responses to the Portrayal of Wolves in Picturebooks (in Evans, J. 2015 *Challenging and Controversial Picturebooks: Children's Responses to Visual Texts*). Kerenza's most recent research study is about stop-motion animation *Prokofiev's Peter & the Wolf* (Templeton, S. 2006), analysed through a posthumanist lens.

Sue Miles-Pearson is Senior Lecturer and Subject lead for Primary Design and Technology Education at the University of Roehampton, London, teaching on both undergraduate and postgraduate programmes. She has worked at Roehampton for sixteen years, and during this time has contributed to D&T publications on food technology and creative teaching in DT.

She has written articles on teaching design and technology in the Early years, and upcycling, recycling and sustainability, and combining control, programming, design and technology to further develop engineering skills. She is a Design and Technology consultant and has spoken about previous articles at two conferences in Birmingham on Computer Aided Design, and Computer Aider Manufacture (CAD CAM) and Design concepts/decisions. Her sessions are as inclusive as possible. Sue is above all a problem-solver and so enjoys new challenges.

Alison Murray leads Primary Physical Education teacher education at the University of Roehampton, where she thrives within a superb team deeply committed to socially just societal engagement. Alison is primary and secondary (US), and secondary (UK) PE trained. She draws from insights into the sensibilities around and through diversity living, from her lived teaching and coaching across the United Kingdom, Mexico and southwest United States. In southwest London, Alison's research is dedicated through collaborative pedagogical efforts, to facilitate the development of pupil autonomy in living a healthy active life.

Susan Ogier is Senior Lecturer in Primary Education, specialising in Art and Design at the University of Roehampton, London. She is author of *Teaching Primary Art and Design* (2017) published by Sage, as well as a series of books for children, professional and peer-reviewed journal articles and book chapters. She is known for her strong association with the subject association NSEAD, and for leading CPD events for class teachers, mentors and senior leaders through consultancy work. She has been involved in several EU funded education research projects focusing on art as a vehicle for learning. Susan's most recently published books in the Learning Matters series are *Teaching the Arts in Primary Schools* (2021), and the second edition of *The Broad and Balanced Curriulum in the Primary School: Educating the Whole Child* (2022).

Bente Opheim is Associate Professor in history at Western Norway University of Applied Sciences. She is an experienced teacher educator and researcher with over twenty years in teachers' education. She has contributed to the development of new national regulations and guidelines for teacher education in Norway. She has also managed several government funded projects exploring teaching methods and learning outcomes in social science and history. She is currently in charge of an extensive in-service master programme for primary and secondary school teachers in Norway.

Gary Pykitt is Senior Lecturer in Primary and Early Years Education at Birmingham City University, teaching professional studies and history. He has also been a history subject leader in a primary school. Gary is currently working towards a Professional Doctorate in Education, focusing on LGBT+ representation and inclusion within primary Relationships Education. Gary is the author of *Shifting Sands: Contemporary Issues in Primary Schools* (Critical Publishing Ltd, 2019). Gary and Damienne Clarke have co-presented primary history workshops around teaching LGBT+ inclusive history for the Historical Association.

Susan Townsend is Senior Lecturer in Primary History and teaches on both primary and secondary PGCE programmes at the University of Roehampton. She is also a Senior Fellow of the Higher Education Academy. She has been in teaching since 1986 with 25 years teaching History in a number of state comprehensive schools, as Head of as well as Head of History. She is also an Ed Excel examiner for the History GCSE. Susan later moved into primary teaching with a special interest in transition from years 6–7 which formed the basis of her MA dissertation. She is passionate about creativity and challenging children to become creative thinkers in their own right. She is a regular contributor to the Historical Association *Primary History Journal* and has run workshops at their annual conferences.

FINDING THE DANCE

I danced into school
Excited to explore,
Looking for bright colours and delight

But then I found …
not numbers swirling into patterns
not words painting pictures

I deconstructed numbers into …
processes and products
I parsed and filleted language …
for the construction blocks of tales

So, I looked to the afternoons, for
Sounds and colours of wonder and
The lure of distant horizons

But then I found …
Where is my voice among the heroes and kings, asked one?
Where are the drums and base notes and the singing sitar, called others?
But no-one wants to know what my place is really like, sighed someone else.
Why do these pictures never show the patterns that I know, enquired another?
And I am not here at all, whispered the last

And so, I knew,
That before I could dance in school
I needed it to change
And hear the music that would speak to all

KJD

"FOREMOST IS A BELIEF IN EDUCATION, AT HOME AND AT SCHOOL, AS A ROUTE TO THE SPIRITUAL, MORAL, SOCIAL, CULTURAL, PHYSICAL AND MENTAL DEVELOPMENT, AND THUS THE WELL-BEING, OF THE INDIVIDUAL. EDUCATION IS ALSO A ROUTE TO EQUALITY OF OPPORTUNITY FOR ALL, A HEALTHY AND JUST DEMOCRACY, A PRODUCTIVE ECONOMY, AND SUSTAINABLE DEVELOPMENT. EDUCATION SHOULD REFLECT THE ENDURING VALUES THAT CONTRIBUTE TO THESE ENDS. THESE INCLUDE VALUING OURSELVES, OUR FAMILIES AND OTHER RELATIONSHIPS, THE WIDER GROUPS TO WHICH WE BELONG, THE DIVERSITY IN OUR SOCIETY AND THE ENVIRONMENT IN WHICH WE LIVE. EDUCATION SHOULD ALSO REAFFIRM OUR COMMITMENT TO THE VIRTUES OF TRUTH, JUSTICE, HONESTY, TRUST AND A SENSE OF DUTY."

NATIONAL CURRICULUM (2000:11)

1
INTRODUCTION

KARIN DOULL

The aim of the book: why this and why now?

Recent years have seen growing popular protests seeking a more equitable and socially just society with movements such as Black Lives Matter, MeToo and Extinction Rebellion. Reports had raised concerns that the underlying issues are not being addressed through education and that there is inequality of representation in curricula, resources and teacher knowledge. The continuing COVID-19 pandemic has highlighted concerns in relation to mental health and identified the importance of social contact and the natural environment. Clearly these are big and complicated issues to consider.

This book does not seek to address all these problems, nor does it have all the answers to the questions these issues pose. The focus here is to present some thoughts about some of the areas that contribute to inequality within our curriculum and suggest some ideas for how to meet these issues within the classroom. While we cannot expect to solve society's ills, we can open aspects of discussion within our classrooms. We can also attempt to create curricula that represent more fairly all aspects of the communities that children live in.

What shapes this text is a belief that children should be able to find themselves and their families in the curriculum that we use in school.

What do we mean by diversity?

In defining the term 'diversity', we can use such words such as diverse, different and varied. While this clearly can shape our understanding, it is also true that this word has more powerful connotations that, when linked to cultural, religious or ethnic categories, have come to relate to opportunity and disadvantage. The 2008 National Curriculum related the term to the need to promote 'racial equality' recognising different past experiences and interpretations. Somers suggests that the term is 'heavily value laden' (2017: 135) and is rarely sufficiently critically analysed. We need to consider how we engage with ideas of diversity, the different, the varied. Do we use this as a mirror to confirm our own perspectives? We need to be aware of the power relationship between the majority view, seen as normative, and a potentially opposing interpretation held by 'the other'. These differences need to be resolved so that collective and individual experiences can be recognised and valued. It is also important to consider the sameness of the human condition, accepting that 'diversity' does not have to suggest the negative. Counsell (in Somers, 2017) suggests that the word complexity could be used instead of diversity. This certainly conveys the multiplicity of issues that might arise in reflecting and analysing human interaction. Multiculturalism recognises and values these many different experiences, demonstrating a sensitivity towards this racial and ethnic diversity. Teaching for diversity allows us to present differences and similarities while also attempting to minimise the power dynamic. It is certainly true that the definitions for multiculturalism and teaching for diversity have many shared aims and sometimes appear interchangeable. What shapes them both is a desire to recognise, value and represent a multiplicity of voice and experiences.

Finding a historical context

The original curriculum authorised in the Education Reform Act 1988 mandated that the curriculum should be 'balanced and broadly based' in order to promote the 'spiritual, moral, cultural, mental and physical development of pupils at the school and of society' and to prepare pupils 'for the opportunities, responsibilities and experiences of adult life' (ERA, 1988: 1). While worthwhile affirmations of intent they did not clarify what they meant by these statements. How did the idea of balanced and broadly based relate to a curriculum that had already designated some subjects as more important (Core) than others (Foundation)? The focus on a 'broad' curriculum did however designate a suite of subjects to which all children were entitled to experience. It was unclear, however, how the competing demands of Core and Foundation subjects might be managed. No definitions for what contributed to 'spiritual, moral, cultural, mental and physical development' were provided. It was not until the 2014 revision that a framework extending and elucidating the philosophy underpinning these key ideas was provided. Key within this document were the ideas of entitlement and diversity.

> *The school curriculum should aim to provide opportunities for all pupils to learn and to achieve.*
>
> (DfEE and QCA, 1999: 11)

This was the first of two aims that shaped the National Curriculum Framework when revised in 1999. It clearly identified the importance of entitlement. This was then further developed in the first of four 'purposes' of the National Curriculum:

> *The National Curriculum secures for all pupils, irrespective of social background, culture, race, gender, differences in ability and disabilities, an entitlement to a number of areas of learning and to develop knowledge, understanding, skills and attitudes necessary for their self-fulfilment and development as active and responsible citizens.*
>
> (DfEE and QCA, 1999: 11)

These two statements inequivalently recognise the need for any curriculum but especially one for the nation, to promote learning that is accessible to all. The concept of *diversity*, linked to personal and community identity, and as an essential consideration in curriculum design shapes this iteration of the English national curriculum. Much of the focus within the aims and purposes related to personal qualities, developed through a series of experiences and linked to developing a sense of personal identity (White, 2004).

┌─────────── **REFLECTION** ───────────┐

On this page you will see an extract from the 'Values and Purposes underpinning the school curriculum' (DfEE and QCA, 1999: 10).

Consider the language that is used here paying particular attention to the words highlighted.

What impression does this give you about those values and purposes?

└──────────────────────────────────────┘

The current national curriculum again reverts to the original aims without providing guidance that would help teachers understand what these requirements mean.

Every state-funded school must offer a curriculum which is balanced and broadly based and which:

- *promotes the spiritual, moral, cultural, mental and physical development of pupils at the school and of society, and*

- *prepares pupils at the school for the opportunities, responsibilities and experiences of later life*

(DfE, 2013: 5)

Across the 163 pages of statutory requirements for the Core subjects, there are no mentions of the words *diversity* or *inclusivity*. These are only explicitly mentioned in history and geography. This naturally suggests that these considerations are no longer central to the broader curriculum design.

┌─────────── **REFLECTION** ───────────┐

Read pages 13–23 in The National Curriculum Framework 1999

http://www.educationengland.org.uk/documents/pdfs/1999-nc-primary-handbook.pdf

and pages 4–11 in the present national curriculum

https://assets.publishing.service.gov.uk/government/uploads/system/uploads/attachment_ data/file/425601/PRIMARY_national_curriculum.pdf

Compare the two documents. What is the same and what is different? What sort of information is provided? How useful is this information? What impression do they give you of the government's thinking or philosophy for education?

└──────────────────────────────────────┘

It is clear, from the demands being raised across society, that education should reflect diverse identities and communities. The present curriculum is perhaps not best suited to this. It is therefore necessary to think of how you might go about adapting the curriculum to reflect these essentials.

REFLECTION

Look at the policy document in relation to social achievement from the social policy document and consider what implications this has.

https://epi.org.uk/wp-content/uploads/2018/07/Wallchart-EPI-2018-Annual-Report-1.pdf

Firstly, it is perhaps useful to consider the different elements that relate to a diverse curriculum. These are linked to the protected characteristics that are to be safeguarded against discrimination. See here for more information: **https://www.equalityhumanrights.com/en/equality-act/protected-characteristics**.

Figure 1.1 below demonstrates issues and concerns impacting vulnerable groups that may be overlooked. We cannot consider all these groups every time we teach but we do need to be aware of them. One way to develop a 'balanced' curriculum is to consider how we might bring aspects of these areas in over the course of a year. Whatever we do needs to be appropriate and valid, or we run the risk of tokenism or superficiality. These aspects will shape the focus of the chapters that follow.

To feel overlooked, misunderstood or ignored either as an individual or a group impacts on our sense of self, of our intrinsic worth (Claire, 2001). We need to consider how far our curriculum links to the

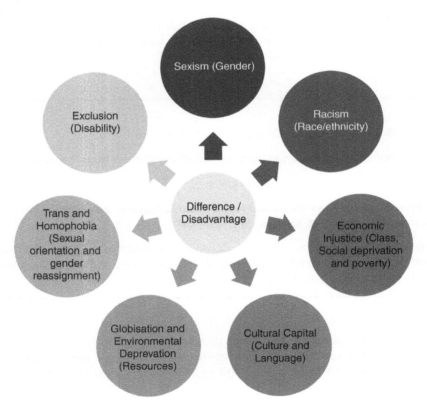

Figure 1.1   Issues and concerns impacting vulnerable groups

reality the children experience and how we help them, to relate to our ideas and ways of working. Diversity within the curriculum relates to pedagogy as well as content.

Identity contains more than one element, and we need to be aware of these multiple or hybrid identities be they racial, geographical, gender or class linked or tied to sexual orientation (Oslar and Starkey, 2000; White, 2004). We all associate ourselves with different groups at different times interacting with cultural and national identities. These too can be seen as multiple and fluid (Figueroa, 2000), constantly requiring new accommodations. In understanding issues relating to diversity and equality, it is important to realise that communities are rarely homogenous (Claire, 2001) or issues of conflict rarely unilateral or simple. The more, we as teachers, seek to understand the issues the more prepared we may be to meet them. It is important to ensure that we know our children, their families and their communities (Claire, 2001). We need to be aware that there may be migrant or immigrant cultures which intersect with the dominant home culture (Korn et al., 2002), white communities with a range of less visible ethnicities (Oslar and Starkey, 2000) and potentially polarised populations who live separate yet parallel lives (Banks, 2009).

Claire suggests that 'identities do not develop in a vacuum but are sustained or undermined through positive or negative experiences in the wider political, economic and social areas' (2001: 49). Schools play a central role in helping children negotiate and develop understanding of who they are. A role in combating inequality is not straight forward or easy. It challenges our own beliefs, creates dissonance, and requires clarity and knowledge (Banks, 1993; Claire, 1996, 2001; Claire et al., 1993; Ramsey et al., 2002). While the focus currently may lie with identifying a Black curriculum and supporting transgender people balancing the needs of other vulnerable groups will also require the same sort of thought and effort.

We began to share the fears of several teachers we met that, with the need for an immediate – even urgent response – to government initiatives, continuing issues such as equal opportunities were in danger of being neglected.

(Claire et al., 1993: 1)

Although this was written almost 30 years ago, there is much that would ring true with teachers today, particularly relating the pressures to respond to government requirements. Sadly, even with growing protest groups in the wider society, the question of equality of opportunity in education still requires consideration. It is true that coping with recent organisational and operational issues and a focus on accountability have marginalised other concerns (Claire et al., 1993; Korn et al., 2002).

The goal remains to provide a curriculum that would enable all to succeed as Samardžić-Marković (2014: 7) suggests to 'bring people together and motivate them to overcome existing dividing lines without creating new ones'. This is not easy to accomplish, however.

For Korn et al. (2002: 4), 'the curriculum is never neutral' maintaining and reflecting the cultural hegemony of the dominant group (Banks, 1993, 2009; Oslar and Starkey, 2000). In addition, children's experiences are shaped not only by their home communities but what they see on social media. Teachers are key curriculum makers with an undertaking to provide experiences to help children interpret their experiences. We are the ones who need to be able to deploy appropriate curriculum content and teaching strategies to create learning opportunities that contest accepted norms, when necessary.

In order to engage with this, we need to have some understanding of the dimensions that might relate to diversity and equality teaching. When working on multicultural education, Banks (1993) suggested a

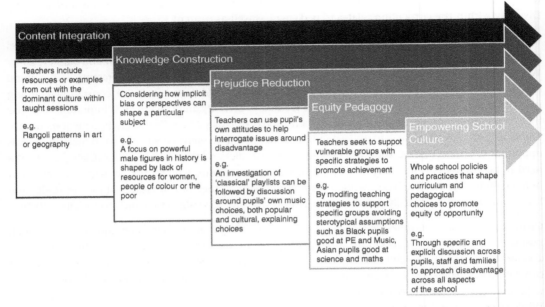

Figure 1.2   Dimensions of multicultural education (Banks, 1993)

number of categories that allow us to consider how far we are moving along the continuum to integrated practice (Figure 1.2).

The following chapters in the book will consider what issues may need to be addressed and consider how they might be approached. Some of the suggestions may be:

- additive – where elements are added to existing curricula, but the structure is not changed

- infusive – where new approaches are threaded through existing content

- transformational – where the structure of the curriculum is changed

- socially active – where children are involved in making choices linked to social change

REFLECTION

Think about teaching music.

- How might you *add* in additional elements to the current music curriculum to make it more diverse?
- What would you like to do to completely *transform* the shape of the music curriculum to represent diversity?
- How could you help children to take part in some *social activism* to lobby the music community to become more representative?

The chapters

Part 1 'Wider dimensions'

The first four chapters set the scene across some of the key areas for consideration. *Chapter 2* considers the Early Years considering how children might be supported in their transition from home to school communities. *Chapters 3* and *4* look at those areas that feature so strongly within national and international debate at the moment, considering race and LGBTQ+ concerns. *Chapter 5* explores multilingual teaching and how to give more prominence to using home languages.

Part 2 'Investigating from other perspectives'

The next three chapters all use history to explore experiences of other perspectives. *Chapter 6* considers why it is still necessary to raise the profile of female achievement within the past. *Chapter 7* looks at how a single household can contain multiple stories of hierarchy, power and remembrance. This is linked to the census returns for a Norwegian family in the 1800s. *Chapter 8* takes a look at 'the other' within us considering some of the perhaps hidden communities that exist in parallel to ours with a particular focus on Irish experiences.

Part 3 'Subject focussed'

This final section of the book takes five different curriculum areas and considers elements of diversity across those subjects, both through content and pedagogy. *Chapter 9* considers our conceptions of place, both local and distant, and how this might be shaped by a dominant narrative. *Chapter 10* suggests aspects of diversity that we might never have considered in relation to what and how we teach physical education (PE), in all its forms. *Chapter 11* investigates visual and sculptural strategies for exploring cultural diversity. *Chapter 12* takes the use of film with children to consider post-humanist representations of story. The final chapter brings together STEM subjects of Design and Technology, Computing and Science to scrutinise some of the hidden biases within those subjects.

Core Curriculum Framework for ITE

Each chapter contains links to the Core Curriculum Framework for ITE (2019) at the beginning. Relevant to this chapter are:

1.1	Teachers have the ability to affect and improve the well-being, motivation and behaviour of their pupils.
1.2	Teachers are key role models, who can influence the attitudes, values and behaviours of their pupils.
1.5	A culture of mutual trust and respect supports effective relationships.
7.2	A predictable and secure environment benefits all pupils.
8.2	Reflective practice, supported by feedback from and observation of experienced colleagues, professional debate and learning from educational research, is also likely to support improvement.

Further reading

BERA blog posts:

https://www.bera.ac.uk/blog-series/education-blacklivesmatter-and-racial-justice-in-the-uk-and-beyond.

https://www.bera.ac.uk/blog/environmental-protest-education-somethings-gone-wrong-somewhere.

https://www.bera.ac.uk/blog/forget-me-not-lgbtiq-representation-and-rights-in-education.

https://www.bera.ac.uk/blog/the-gender-wars-academic-freedom-and-education.

https://www.bera.ac.uk/blog-series/wellbeing-being-outdoors.

References

Banks, J. (1993) Multicultural education: historical development, dimensions and practice. *Review of Research in Education, 19*: 3–49.

Banks, J. (ed.) (2009) *The Routledge International Companion to Multicultural Education.* Abingdon: Routledge.

Claire, H. (1996) *Reclaiming Our Pasts: Equality and Diversity in the Primary History Curriculum.* Stoke on Trent: Trentham Books.

Claire, H. (2001) *We Are Not Aliens: Primary Children and the Citizenship/PHSE Curriculum.* Stoke on Trent: Trentham Books.

Claire, H., Maybin, J. and Swann, J. (1993) *Equality Matters.* Clevedon: Multilingual Matters Ltd.

DfEE and QCA (1999) *The National Curriculum Framework.* Available at: **https://www.educationengland.org.uk/documents/pdfs/1999-nc-primary-handbook.pdf** (accessed 22 August 2021)

DfE (2013) *The National Curriculum in England.* Available at: **https://assets.publishing.service.gov.uk/government/uploads/system/uploads/attachment_data/file/425601/PRIMARY_national_curriculum.pdf** (accessed 22 August 2021)

Figueroa, P. (2000) Citizenship education for a plural society. In A. Oslar (ed.), *Citizenship and Diversity in Schools: Identity, Equality.* Stoke on Trent: Trentham Books.

Korn, E., Burgztyn, A. and Kinchloe, J. (2002) *Rethinking Multicultural Education: Case Studies in Cultural Transition.* London: Greenwood Publishing Group Inc.

Oslar, A. and Starkey, H. (2000) Citizenship, human rights and cultural diversity. In A. Oslar (ed.), *Citizenship and Diversity in Schools: Identity, Equality.* Stoke on Trent: Trentham Books.

Ramsey, P., Williams, L.R. and Vold, E. (2002) *Multicultural Education: A Source Book*, 2nd edition. London: Taylor and Francis.

Samardzic-Markovic, S. (2014) *Shared Histories for a Europe Without Dividing Lines.* Available at: **https://rm.coe.int/shared-histories-for-a-europe-without-dviding-lines/1680994a97** (accessed 18 April 2022)

Somers, R. (2017) Unmasking diversity: curriculum rhetoric meets the classroom. In Counsell, et al. (eds), *Masterclass in History Education*. London: Bloomsbury, pp. 135–149.

The Education Reform Act. (1988) *c2*. Available at: **https://www.legislation.gov.uk/ukpga/ 1988/40/contents** (accessed 18 April 2022)

White, J. (ed.) (2004) *Rethinking the School Curriculum*. London: Routledge Falmer.

2
EMBRACING DIVERSE PERSPECTIVES IN THE EARLY YEARS

HELEN CRAWFORD

KEYWORDS: COMMUNITIES; CULTURE; DIVERSITY; ENVIRONMENTS; EYFS; IDENTITY; PAST; PEOPLE; PLACES; STEREOTYPES

CHAPTER OBJECTIVES

The aims of this chapter are:

- To understand the importance of a diverse curriculum within Early Years education.
- To provide examples of how to embed diverse and inclusive perspectives within the EYFS curriculum.

CCF ITE links

	Learn that:	Learn how to:
1.2	Teachers are key role models, who can influence the attitudes, values and behaviours of their pupils.	Use intentional and consistent language that promotes challenge and aspiration.
2.1	Learning involves a lasting change in pupils' capabilities or understanding.	Identify possible misconceptions and plan how to prevent these forming.

	Learn that:	Learn how to:
3.7	In all subject areas, pupils learn new ideas by linking those ideas to existing knowledge, organising this knowledge into increasingly complex mental models (or 'schemata').	Identify essential concepts, knowledge, skills and principles of the subject [area of learning].

Introduction

Education needs to enable the student to look through window frames in order to see the realities of others and into mirrors in order to see her/his own reality reflected. Knowledge of both types of framing is basic to a balanced education.

(Style, 1988)

This chapter will explore how the flexibility and freedom of the Early Years Foundation Stage (EYFS) framework (DfE, 2021a) offers Early Years practitioners opportunities to create and shape a curriculum that can encompass diverse perspectives. With a focus on the specific area of 'Understanding the World', Style's (1988) view of curriculum as both mirror and window provides a framework for creating an effective Early Years curriculum. As a mirror, the curriculum should reflect the child's emerging sense of self, family and community. As a window, it should reveal the past, the people and the places beyond the child's immediate experiences. This is crucial at a time when young children are beginning to establish a sense of their own identity and to form opinions, views and perspectives of the wider world.

Children's developing understanding of themselves

Good practice in the Early Years classroom needs to build on and respond to children's earliest formative experiences and acknowledge their own funds of both knowledge and identity (Esteban-Guitart and Moll, 2014). The latter is defined as the 'historically accumulated, culturally developed and socially distributed resources that are essential for a person's self-definition, self-expression and self-understanding' (Esteban-Guitart and Moll, 2014: 31). Identity formation is complex, involving the intersection of categories such as gender, social class, ethnicity or disability (Siraj-Blatchford, 2014). It emerges from both a child's everyday experiences as well as their formal learning and is 'a dynamic composite of who we are and who we are becoming' (Esteban-Guitart and Moll, 2014: 44).

Effective communication with parents/carers as children transition into formal Early Years education is therefore essential; information sharing allows practitioners to plan for and build upon children's prior experiences and interests (DfE, 2021a). In this way the curriculum can be connected to and mirror a child's culture, value systems and emerging identity (Esteban-Guitart and Moll, 2014). Teaching and learning experiences should then be designed to help children become explicitly aware of their different multi-faceted identities, as this awareness may make them more positively attuned to the different identities of others (Siraj-Blatchford, 2014). This involves careful curriculum planning to ensure that selected resources include a range of diverse perspectives that may reflect the child's own emerging identity and set of values (DfE, 2021b).

REFLECTION

Think back to your own childhood. What values were important to your family? How do you know? How have they shaped your identity?

Challenging stereotypes

As children develop, they subconsciously form preconceptions about the world based on what they see and experience. They develop schema – mental frameworks – that help them to organise their thinking and ideas. These categories of knowledge begin to define their understanding of what is 'the norm' in relation to a given group. They can therefore become limiting as children form stereotypes – based on attributing features to a particular group and inferring that all members should possess such features.

As children build up more detailed understandings of the world, their schemas become increasingly complex. They expand as children accommodate and assimilate new information (Halfpenny and Petterson, 2014). Children's views on gender differences, for example, have been shown to be more 'fixed' or rigid at a young age, but become increasingly nuanced and flexible with maturity (Martin and Ruble, 2010). Teachers are important role models who can inform and influence the attitudes and behaviours of their pupils (DFE, 2019a: 9). Early Years practitioners need therefore to consider carefully how they can support children's development of increasingly complex mental models of people and places. This can help to minimise reductive or tokenistic perceptions of what is considered 'the norm' and avoid what Adichie (2009) has referred to as a 'single story' of people and places.

REFLECTION

Think of any stereotypes linked to different groups in our society. Are they positive or negative? How might these stereotypes be limiting – both for ourselves and for others?

Effective enabling environments

One of the key principles of the EYFS framework is the importance of enabling environments – environments that are rich and varied and support children's learning and development (DfE, 2021a). Enabling environments can encompass the actual space of the setting (both indoor and outdoor), the support and guidance provided by adults, but also the resources that are made available to children. This includes the resources used for adult-led activities as well as those that are made available for child-initiated activities as part of a setting's continuous provision.

Play is considered to be at the heart of good Early Years pedagogy and practice. It is essential for children's development 'building their confidence as they learn to explore, relate to others, set their own goals and solve problems' (DfE, 2021a: 16). Both indoor and outdoor learning environments should give children opportunities to develop and sustain their own interests through their choice of play. This is important for children as a means of developing their own identity as learners and to learn to appreciate similarities and differences between themselves and their peer group. Practitioners should therefore consider the types of resources they provide for children and how they might limit or expand children's worldviews. Development Matters (the non-statutory guidance for EYFS practitioners), for example, recommends that Early Years settings provide books and play materials that reflect the diversity of life in modern Britain, positive images of people who are disabled and materials that will confront and challenge gender stereotypes (DfE, 2021b).

Children's developing understanding of the past, people and places

For children from disadvantaged homes, active participation in school may be the only opportunity that they have to acquire powerful knowledge and be able to move, intellectually at least, beyond their local and their particular circumstances.

(Young, 2008: 15)

The EYFS framework (DfE, 2021a) is premised on the holistic development of the child. It is designed to facilitate a curriculum that is inter-connected, centred around seven areas of learning and development (Table 2.1):

Table 2.1 EYFS framework: areas of learning and development

The prime areas:	The specific areas:
• Communication and language • Physical development • Personal, social and emotional development	• Literacy • Mathematics • Understanding the world • Expressive arts and design

Source: DfE (2021a).

The framework is deliberately flexible, to provide practitioners with the freedom to design a curriculum which best responds to their children's needs. The specific area 'Understanding the World' emphasises the importance of how children begin to make sense of the physical world and their community (DfE, 2021a). Within this area, there is an explicit emphasis upon the importance of providing children with real life experiences:

The frequency and range of children's personal experiences increases their knowledge and sense of the world around them – from visiting parks, libraries and museums to meeting important members of society such as police officers, nurses and firefighters.

(DfE, 2021a: 10)

Everyday experiences can enhance children's understanding of their world as they identify patterns and connections between what they see, engage with and experience. While some Early Years settings may have limited resources and/or capacity to fund wider explorations of the world, consistent engagement with the local community helps children to develop their relationships with others and is a means to address potential disadvantage in children's starting points (Forrester et al., 2021). This develops children's social and cultural capital as they encounter people from different walks of life, of different generations and from different backgrounds (Forrester et al., 2021). Effective community engagement integrates the personal and social and, in doing so, opens up a child's windows on to the world.

REFLECTION

Think of a school setting you know well. What opportunities are there to engage with the local community? What would be the value of this engagement for children?

Exploring past and present

The Early Learning Goals (ELGs) are the knowledge, skills and understanding children should have at the end of their Reception year and are closely aligned with distinct subject disciplines (DfE, 2021a). Within 'Understanding the World', the ELG *'Past and Present'* expects children by the end of their Reception year to be able to:

- talk about the lives of the people around them and their roles in society;

- know some similarities and differences between things in the past and now, drawing on their experiences and what has been read in class;

- understand the past through settings, characters and events encountered in books read in class and storytelling.

(DFE, 2021a)

For young children, their first encounter with history will be their own history. Asking children to bring in photographs of themselves as a baby or toddler helps them to make connections between their past and their present. It is a meaningful introduction to similarity and difference – two of the second order concepts in history – and also to the value of images as primary sources of evidence (Kirkland, 2017). Comparing and sequencing images also enable children to develop an emergent understanding of chronology which is a key mechanism for framing our understanding of the past (Clarke, 2020). However, while focusing on the history of their own family can reaffirm a child's sense of their own identity, this should be negotiated with care when supporting any child with challenging or vulnerable personal circumstances.

Speaking and listening activities designed to explore family narratives also provide an effective way for children to understand the value of oral history as a source of evidence about the past.

There are also opportunities here for children to make comparisons and to explore how their family story is different from, or similar to, those of their peer group. This introduces children to the idea that there are multiple and diverse ways to be a family – a principle that is foregrounded in the Relationships Education statutory guidance (DfE, 2019b). A focus on both the self and others also prepares children for the primary National Curriculum for history, which states that history should contribute to pupils' understanding of both their own identity and diversity within society (DfE, 2013).

Exploring people, culture and communities

Within 'Understanding the World', the ELG *'People, Culture and Communities'* expects children by the end of their Reception year to be able to:

- describe their immediate environment using knowledge from observation, discussion, stories, non-fiction texts and maps;

- know some similarities and differences between different religious and cultural communities in this country, drawing on their experiences and what has been read in class;

- explain some similarities and differences between life in this country and life in other countries, drawing on knowledge from stories, non-fiction texts and – when appropriate – maps.

(DFE, 2021a)

Modern Britain is increasingly secular and pluralistic, encompassing a range of worldviews (CORE, 2018). Learning about others invites children to consider what personal or community experiences are important to themselves and their family. This contributes not just towards their own personal, social and emotional development (PSED) but also to an appreciation of British Values such as religious tolerance and individual liberty (DfE, 2014). In a multicultural and diverse society, classrooms where children can learn from each other can be an effective way to challenge misconceptions (Catling and Willy, 2018; James and Stern, 2019). Early Years practitioners should consider how to create opportunities to invite visitors from religious or cultural communities into their settings and to ensure that the curriculum timetable is structured to encompass learning about seasonal traditions, festivals or celebrations, such as Diwali or Eid (DfE, 2021b).

Learning related to geography involves working at a range of scales, encompassing the local, the national and the global. Young children first begin to develop a sense of their personal geographies through the places and spaces which are important for them and their family. As they begin to compare their own lives with life in other places in the world, practitioners need to go beyond asking children to draw similarities and differences between 'here' and 'there'; there should be a more nuanced focus on similarities and differences within localities, not just across them (Catling and Willy, 2018). This will help to minimise any stereotypes about particular places or communities. Resources, such as images of places beyond the child's immediate personal experience, should therefore be selected with care to ensure that they do not tell just a 'single story' (Adichie, 2009). Exposure to a range of books – both fiction and non-fiction – is also a key part of a rich learning environment and is foregrounded in the EYFS framework (DfE, 2021a). Picture books can be used to introduce children to complex issues such as interdependence, migration, diversity and social justice in a way that is accessible for even the youngest children (Dolan, 2016).

Case study

Coming to England by Floella Benjamin (2020) is a picture book based on the author's early childhood. Floella and her family belong to the Windrush generation, those who arrived in the United Kingdom from Caribbean countries between 1948 and 1971. *Coming to England* tells the story of Floella's journey from the island of Trinidad to London in 1960. The book encapsulates a range of themes which can be used as a stimulus for including diverse perspectives in relation to teaching about the past, people, culture and communities. Here are some ideas (Figures 2.1 and 2.2):

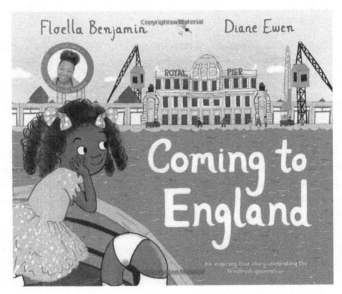

Figure 2.1   Coming to England by Floella Benjamin (Source: ***https://www.panmacmillan.com/authors/floella-benjamin/coming-to-england/9781529009415***).

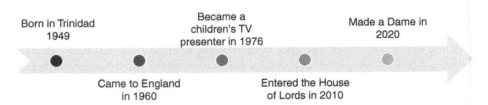

Figure 2.2   Timeline

EYFS area of learning and development	Theme	Activities and key questions
Understanding the World	Past Present Family	Visit **https://www.barnardos.org.uk/oral-history-project/floella-benjamin** Look at the photos of Floella when she was a child. Listen to her describe her childhood. Discuss with children how photos (images) and listening to people (oral history) are effective ways to learn about what life was like for different people in the past. Make a timeline showing the different events in Floella' s life. Add to the timeline different images of Floella at different stages of her life. Mark all the decades in Floella life. Add to the timeline images of other important events in different decades (e.g. the moon landing of 1969). You could also add key events or anniversaries in the history of your school or local area. Ask the children to make their own timeline showing important events in their lives. *Key Questions:* Which times in Floella's life have been the happiest or the saddest? Why? How are our own timelines different from each other? How are they similar?
Understanding the World Personal, Social and Emotional Development (PSED)	Family Communication Past Present	Discuss how Floella and her parents communicated by writing letters. Provide writing paper and envelopes in the graphics area and materials for making stamps. Ask the children to write letters to their own family members. *Key Questions:* What do you think Floella wrote in her letters to her parents? What do you think her parents told Floella about life in England? What are all the different ways we communicate with our families today (e.g. video calls, birthday cards)? What is your favourite way to communicate with your friends and family, especially those who live far away?
Understanding the World	Empire Monarchy Migration Transport Past Present	Find Trinidad and England on a globe or atlas. Explain to the children about the British Empire and the links between the United Kingdom and other places in the world. For example, look at the flag of Trinidad (and Tobago) in 1960, linking the Union Jack on that flag to the flag of the United Kingdom. Compare with the flag of Trinidad today. Look at familiar images of Queen Elisabeth II (e.g. on coins or stamps). Discuss the role of the queen in the story as an important figure in Floella's life. Consider why families and people might move from one place to another place. Collect images to show the different ways we used to travel long distances and the ways we travel today. *Key Questions:* Why did Floella and her family decide to leave Trinidad to come to England? How do you think Floella felt on the long journey? Do you know anyone who has moved from one place to live in another place? Why did they move? How did they travel?

(Continued)

(Continued)

EYFS area of learning and development	Theme	Activities and key questions
PSED	Diversity Ethnicity Racism	Discuss with the children what happened to Floella when she started school in London. Share all the ways we look similar to each other and all the way we look different from each other. Make a class display of self-portraits celebrating our differences and similarities. *Key Questions:* Why were children in her school unkind? How do you think that made Floella feel? What are the different ways we can show kindness to other children in our class? What are the different ways we can show kindness to other people we meet?
Understanding the World	Place knowledge Contrasting localities	Compare and contrast the physical and human geography of Trinidad and London. Compare the wet and hot season in Trinidad with the four seasons of autumn, winter, spring and summer in England. Look at the market scene and name all the different fruits. Which fruits are grown in Trinidad? Which of these fruits can we buy today in England? How are they transported here? Which fruits can we grow in England? Set up a fruit and vegetable stall in the role-play area. Have a tasting session – which fruits do they prefer? *Key Questions:* Which pictures in the book show Trinidad? How do you know? Which pictures in the book show England? How do you know? What is the weather like in each country? What clothes do people wear?

CHAPTER SUMMARY

This chapter has argued for the importance of including diverse perspectives when teaching young children. The flexible nature of the EYFS framework and the freedoms embedded within the seven areas of learning and development mean that there is considerable scope for practitioners to devise learning experiences which value children's own funds of identity (Esteban and Moll, 2014) and the formative experiences they bring into the classroom. This should be the foundation for developing children's emergent sense of the world around them, at a range of scales and involving a range of perspectives. Classroom resources should be designed to respond to children's interests and should be selected to ensure positive approaches to diversity. Early Years practitioners need to plan for a wide range of learning experiences both within and beyond the classroom, enabling children to encounter peoples, places and communities beyond their own. In this way, the curriculum can become both a mirror and a window (Style, 1988), reflecting the child's reality and opening up the realities of others.

References

Adichie, C. (2009) *The Danger of a Single Story.* TEDGlobal. **https://www.ted.com/talks/chimamanda_ngozi_adichie_the_danger_of_a_single_story?language=zh**.

Catling, S. and Willy, T. (2018) *Understanding and Teaching Primary Geography,* 2nd edition. London: SAGE.

Clarke, D. (2020) Developing chronological understanding and language in the early years and foundation stage. *Primary History, 86:* 14–17.

CORE (2018) *Religion and Worldviews: The Way Forward – A National Plan for RE.* **https://www.religiouseducationcouncil.org.uk/wp-content/uploads/2017/05/Final-Report-of-the-Commission-on-RE.pdf**.

DfE (2013) *The National Curriculum in England: Key Stages 1 and 2 Framework Document.* London: DfE.

DfE (2014) *Promoting Fundamental British Values as Part of SMSC in Schools Departmental Advice for Maintained Schools.* London: DfE.

DfE (2019a) *ITT Core Content Framework.* London: DfE.

DfE (2019b) *Relationships Education, Relationships and Sex Education (RSE) and Health Education Statutory Guidance for Governing Bodies, Proprietors, Head Teachers, Principals, Senior Leadership Teams, Teachers.* London: DfE.

DfE (2021a) *Statutory Framework for the Early Years Foundation Stage.* London: DfE.

DfE (2021b) *Development Matters Non-Statutory Curriculum Guidance for the Early Years Foundation Stage.* London: DfE.

Dolan, A. (2016) Engaging with the world through picture books. In S. Scoffham (ed.), *Teaching Geography Creatively.* London: Routledge, pp. 30–43. **https://doi.org/10.4324/9781315667775**.

Esteban-Guitart, M. and Moll, L.C. (2014) Funds of identity: a new concept based on the funds of knowledge approach. *Culture & Psychology, 20*(1): 31–48. **https://doi.org/10.1177/1354067X13515934**.

Forrester, G. Pugh, J. Hudson, R. and Rowley, J. (2021) Understanding the world in the early years foundation stage: practitioners' perspectives of best practice and effective provision. *Education, 3–13:* 1–13. **https://doi.org/10.1080/03004279.2021.1930095**.

Halfpenny, A.M. and Pettersen, J. (2014) *Introducing Piaget. A Guide for Practitioners and Students in Early Years Education.* London: Routledge.

James, M. and Stern, J. (2019) *Mastering Primary Religious Education.* London: Bloomsbury Academic.

Kirkland, S. (2017) Learning about the past through 'ourselves and our families'. *Primary History, 75:* 6–7.

Martin, C.L. and Ruble, D.N. (2010) Patterns of gender development. *Annual Review of Psychology, 61*(1): 353–381. **https://doi.org/10.1146/annurev.psych.093008.100511**.

Siraj-Blatchford, I. (2014) Diversity, inclusion and learning in the early years. In G. Pugh and B. Duffy (eds), *Contemporary Issues in the Early Years,* 6th edition. London: SAGE, pp. 181–198.

Style, E. (1988) Curriculum as window and mirror. In *Listening for All Voices.* Summit, NJ: Oak Knoll School Monograph.

Young, M. (2008) From constructivism to realism in the sociology of the curriculum. *Review of Research in Education, 32*(1): 1–28. **https://doi.org/10.3102/0091732X07308969**.

3

THE TEACHING OF HISTORY AS A VEHICLE FOR CHANGE

SUSIE TOWNSEND

WE MAY HAVE DIFFERENT RELIGIONS, DIFFERENT LANGUAGES, DIFFERENT COLOURED SKIN, BUT WE ALL BELONG TO ONE HUMAN RACE.

KOFI ANNAN

KEYWORDS: CRITICAL RACE THEORY; DECOLONISATION; EMPIRE; IDENTITY; MULTICULTURALISM; UNCONSCIOUS BIAS; WORLD WAR

CHAPTER OBJECTIVES

The aims of this chapter are:

- To review the present History curriculum in terms of racial diversity.
- To reflect on Black History Month and Black Lives Matter and their impact.
- To explore British history from differing racial perspectives; recognising hidden voices and achievements.
- To consider potential issues when developing a school history curriculum map and how they might be overcome.
- To provide examples of activities that can be used in the classroom which embrace and reflect our multicultural society.

CCF ITE links

1.2	Teachers are key role models, who can influence the attitudes, values and behaviours of their pupils.
2.1	Learning involves a lasting change in pupils' capabilities or understanding.
3.1	A school's curriculum enables it to set out its vision for the knowledge, skills and values that its pupils will learn, encompassing the national curriculum within a coherent wider vision for successful learning.

Introduction

Identity is the history that has gone into bone and blood and reshaped the flesh. Identity is not what we were but what we have become what we are at this moment.

(Nick Joaquin, 1988)

History shapes our own identity as an individual and helps us understand ourselves and our place within the 'long arc of development'. Britain is a multicultural society; In 2011, Leicester was the first city in the United Kingdom where the majority of the residents identified themselves as non-white British. But is this racial diversity reflected in the history that is taught in the classroom?

Politically, history also defines our national identity and there are tensions between the two. The constructed view of the past of our nation needs to be held to account and questioned and be challenged by individual histories. This national identity needs to be a collective one where every group in our society has a voice that can be heard. In the Census 2021, 8 million people (14% of the population) identified as form a Black, Asian or mixed multi-ethnic group, but are their histories reflected in our nation's narrative (DfE FE Commission, 2020)?

This chapter considers the ongoing debate surrounding diversity, the content of the History National Curriculum (NC) and what and how history is taught. The impact of the Black Lives Matter movement is discussed and initiatives such as Black History Month. The focus of the chapter is on the need for children to understand that there are different stories and perspectives and hidden voices that need to be heard while suggesting ways that this could be promoted in the classroom.

What is meant by critical race theory and decolonising the curriculum?

Critical Race Theory (CRT) is an understanding that society is 'shaped by racism which is endemic, systematic and often unrecognised' (Bradbury, 2020: 243). It considers that policies and curricula can be fundamentally prejudiced against minority groups. Often this is not the intention, and policies may seem to be 'colourblind' but in fact have racial consequences. Decolonising the curriculum has its basis in this theory:

Decolonizing the curriculum means creating spaces and resources for a dialogue among all members of the university on how to imagine and envision all cultures and knowledge systems in the curriculum, and with respect to what is being taught and how it frames the world.

(Keele University Manifesto, cited by Charles, 2019: 1)

This useful definition clarifies what is meant by decolonising the curriculum. Students have put pressure on universities to review the curriculum that is offered and to make sure that the views of all are represented, and there is equality in the system, the processes and the staffing of the university. Discussions about this begun in 1990s but have gained real momentum following the creation of the Black Lives Matter movement in 2013 and its transformation into a worldwide phenomenon following the death of George Floyd in 2020. It is with this background of change that the History NC should be measured against to see if it promotes equality and diversity or militates against it.

REFLECTION

What do you understand by the term 'decolonizing the curriculum'? How might this relate to across the curriculum?

So how diverse is the History National Curriculum as a policy?

The various iterations of the History NC demonstrate a change in emphasis about diversity within the History Curriculum; in 2008 History Curriculum, diversity was defined as a statutory concept – cultural, ethnic and religious diversity (QCA, 2008). The attainments target all referred to the need to consider history within a local, national and international framework and, within that, to analyse the nature and extent of diversity. This would indicate that diversity was considered important by the policymakers of the time although there was also criticism that the multicultural perspective of the NC was tokenistic (Dennis, 2016; Bracey et al., 2011).

In contrast, the 2013 History NC only makes one specific reference in the purpose of study:

*History helps pupils to understand the complexity of people's lives, the process of change, the **diversity** of societies and relationships between different groups, as well as their own identity and the challenges of their time.*

(DfE 2014: 1)

The *History Review* (2021) also only mentions diversity once in a section related to the breadth of the curriculum offer, with an example from Wilkinson about the importance of Islamic boys knowing about Islamic civilisations and the following statement:

Moreover, the national curriculum refers not only to diverse pasts but to the importance of history in developing pupils' identities. In modern multi-cultural Britain, pupils' community pasts are diverse and often blended and complex.

(*History Review*, 2021)

Although there are ways in which the History Curriculum can represent diverse views, it is clear that the policy does not emphasise this and it is diversity by default rather than intent. The NC is strongly criticised in the Black Curriculum Report 2021 for presenting a White Anglocentric view of history which fails to represent or ignores other viewpoints.

So does the actual content in history at Key Stages 1 and 2 allow for an appreciation of racial diversity and identity?

At Key Stage 1, the four units do not mention diversity, and there is no requirement to do so; it is left up to schools and teachers to implement if they wish. Rather than insisting on the incorporation of world and diverse histories at the core of the discipline, this means that schools can opt out of choices and present a broadly white male insular view of British history (Alexander et al., 2012). There are opportunities to build diversity into the curriculum (see the section on teaching ideas and strategies) but they rely on schools making the decision to do this and on teachers having the confidence and subject knowledge to carry this out effectively. The non-statutory guidance does not specifically promote this. For example, in suggested content for the unit on significant individuals, there are a list of thirteen possible suggestions; when viewing these in terms of diversity, five are from outside the United Kingdom and two are people of colour – Mary Seacole and Rosa Parks. There are no racially diverse examples from the United Kingdom itself.

At Key Stage 2, out of the nine units that are taught, three of them are based on wider world history; early civilisations, ancient Greece and a non-European society unit. A fourth is about the Roman Empire but the focus needs to be on its impact on Britain. The other units are British-centric although there is potential here for Black and Asian links. The theme beyond 1066 is open to choice. But what are schools choosing? The lack of the much loved Tudors and Victorians in the Key Stage 2 curriculum means that many schools use this unit as a way of delivering some history on one of those time periods.

This NC is for schools in England and so it is natural and right that children should learn history about the country that they live in and every country in the world will have their own focus. However, history is about analysing and debating, interpreting, questioning and above all challenging. There must be an awareness of the wider world and a recognition of different viewpoints about events and people. There must also be an understanding that British people can have different heritages, that we have a collective history, and everyone's story is a vital part of the history of our country – history is about people and the society in which they live and hidden voices need to be heard and their contributions celebrated (Osler, 2009).

Phillips (2002) asserted that a focus on diversity in history teaching can lead to children gaining a more inclusive view of society and a more informed outward view of the world. History teaching should reflect the cultures and backgrounds of all children and allow them to explore and understand their own identity and deepen their understanding of others; by engaging children in the global view teachers will begin to break down the barriers that can exist in the curriculum and teach children to recognise and tolerate different perspectives.

Is it time for Black History Month to evolve?

The idea of celebrating Black History was the brainchild of Carter G Woodson, a Black historian who began Black History week in 1926, but its conception, in the format that is current today, was devised at Kent University in 1970. The purpose of the event was to raise awareness of African/Caribbean Americans and their history during the month of February and has now spread to other countries. It was first celebrated in Britain in 1987 and takes place in October. It has been a vehicle for change in many schools in the United Kingdom as this explicit focus on Black History and its significance has led to the celebration of positive Black British role models rather than focusing on Black History as being just about one story – slavery.

There are issues with this approach, however, and debate about whether there should be change. There are many other ethnic groups that have played a vital part in the development of Britain as a nation, for example, the legacy of empire has meant that there may be a need for more explicit emphasis on Asian communities and their contributions. In a climate of political correctness, many teachers are unsure if they should include other racial groups under the banner of Black History. For example, it has been evident that people of Chinese descent have suffered from a huge rise in racial comments and abuse as a consequence of the COVID pandemic but their views and contributions to our community seem to be hidden from public view (**https://www.itv.com/news/2021-07-16/uk-chinese-people-may-be-scarred-for-more-than-a-generation-after-virus-abuse**). To consider their history under the umbrella of Black History would be a misnomer so perhaps it is time to expand the definition of Black History Month.

There can also be the view that a box has been ticked, and Black History has been 'done' in October and does not need to be revisited again; there is a need to integrate diversity into the whole history curriculum so that it is not an 'add on' but an essential. However, there is a danger that without Black History Month as a flagship the focus on diversity will be diluted and lose momentum.

The seminal Swann Report made such an observation when stating

> multicultural understanding has to permeate all aspects of a school's work. It is not a separate practice that can be welded onto existing practices.
>
> (Swann Report, 1985: 10)

Refocusing on the term 'diversity', rather than Black History, as a key aspect of the curriculum could help reinforce the view that everyone's identity is unique and needs to be reflected in what is being taught and that it should be interwoven throughout the whole school curriculum. Other groups in society need to be acknowledged too, such as those of different class, gender, disability or sexuality as well as other races. Maybe this is the next stage of development in terms of appreciating different cultural heritage.

REFLECTION

What evidence of Black History have you seen in school? Has this been embedded in the curriculum or some sort of 'add on'?

What are the issues in including diversity in a school curriculum map and how might they be resolved?

In the key findings of the *Curriculum Review: Diversity and Citizenship* (2007) Ajebo et al. identified a number of factors which were limiting the drive to a diverse curriculum. These included low prioritisation by school leaders, lack of training, lack of confidence by teachers and lack of resources and where to access them. These inhibiting factors continued to be highlighted specifically in the *History Curriculum* (Harris and Clarke, 2011).

The changes in teacher training have led to a government shift away from universities to more school-based routes. This does lead inevitably to less time for trainee teachers to build subject knowledge and pedagogy especially in primary schools where the emphasis on literacy and numeracy has led in many schools to a narrowed curriculum. The amount of time allocated for foundation subjects in primary teacher training is usually very limited and even more so where there is less history expertise available. There is also not the time to unpick the curriculum and consider how the units could be made more diverse.

This lack of training and potentially of subject knowledge leads to a lack of confidence in even experienced teachers. Many teachers recognise the importance of diversity but are worried about how they might do this and if they might use the wrong words or cause offence through a lack of their own understanding. As Alexander et al. (2012: 15) commented:

> Diversity is seen as controversial and 'personal', and freighted with emotional baggage which they [the teachers] feel they lack the subject expertise to deal with.

There has been some progress, however. The focus of the Ofsted Education Inspection Framework (EIF) 2021 has emphasised the need for an ambitious, inclusive curriculum and for the broad range of subjects to be taught. In primary schools, this has led to a refocusing on foundation subjects how they are taught. There is also reference to learners 'developing their understanding and appreciation of diversity' although this is linked specifically to British values and stresses commonality rather than difference. Nevertheless the EIF does encourage school leaders to justify and provide a rationale for their curriculum map.

In terms of training, this inspection framework has also focused Initial Teacher Training (ITT) providers on the need for an ambitious programme of study which should be continued into the first two years of teaching and beyond. Teachers need Continual Professional Development (CPD) so that they can gain confidence in how they can make the History Curriculum more diverse and resources that are available to support them. However, the Early Career Framework (ECF) 2019 has no specific references to the importance of diversity and no specific resources for history as a subject area. Neither is there a specific reference to diversity in the Core Content Framework (CCF) which is the curriculum that ITT providers are being assessed against. It would seem that although the importance of recognising and celebrating racial diversity has become much more evident in the media through movements such as Black Lives Matter, this does not seem to have been reflected in all recent government legislation.

How well prepared do you feel to plan and teach across a diverse curriculum? What additional support might you need?

Case study

How to make Key Stage 1 more diverse?

Here are two of the units that are taught and some suggestions about how integration of racial diversity could be achieved.

Who are you? Draw around each child so that there is an outline and then draw a timeline within the outline showing each year of the child's life. Get them to think of key events in their own life, such as the birth of a sibling or a new pet for the family. It could be when they got a special present or went on holiday. Speak to parent and ask for photos which would be stuck within the outline at the correct point on the timeline. They could then have a circle around their outline with things that have happened locally/nationally and then another circle for events that are international. In this way, they can see how their identity is part of a collective identity.

A theme within living memory – you could look at a decade such as the 1950s or 1960s when their grandparents might have been born. You could look at the Windrush generation and the influx of Indian migration. Children could consider push and pull factors and then look at sources to gain an idea about what it was like to arrive in a new country and what they brought with them. A theme like this could also provide the focus for a significant event – The birth of the Notting Hill Carnival, for example, in 1966 or the landing on the moon in 1969. A topic such as this has many cross curricular links. Fashion, music, technology, architecture, art are just a few of the areas to be explored. Who were the famous artists at the time, what style of art was popular and why? Who were famous poets and writers of children books? A typical 1960s meal could be created or a cut-out paper doll with clothes that you could attach using tabs. Children could create a dance to show the arrival of the Windrush or a fashion show catwalk. Linking history and geography they could put pins in 10 random places around the world. Where have they landed? What is that place like? What was happening there in the 1960s?

In terms of historical events, the space race would provide links to scientific developments, and an understanding of the work of hidden figures such as Mary Jackson, Katherine Johnson and Dorothy Vaughan would demonstrate the significance of a team of individuals in making journeys to the moon a reality. The 1960s is a period of protest and fights for equality so the Civil Rights Movement, the Bristol Bus Boycott, LGBT and discrimination against Native American and Aboriginal people are all ideas that could be explored although these may be more appropriate if looking at the 1960s at Key Stage 2. The Vietnam War would also be better studied at Key Stage 2. There is so much that you could explore with this decade. Most importantly, however, the children could ask their families about their own stories from the time.

Significant individuals – The NC states that you must study at least two individuals and compare them so that their achievements are in the context of the period. A class can study as many individuals as they would like and again there are opportunities to really expand children's knowledge and look outward to the wider world. Considering a theme such as explorers or scientists or famous artists could allow children to place the individuals chronologically and consider continuity and change but will also link to other areas of the curriculum. They can come from different parts of the world, different time periods and from different racial backgrounds. Children could be asked to find out about someone who they wanted to find out about from their own cultural background. It could be part of a show-and-tell session or it could be linked to anniversaries of individuals or an investigation about the Google Doodle for the day. They could indeed produce their own Google Doodle but again outcomes can be cross curricular – they could create a 3D object for the museum shop to sell which tell people about the person and what they did and includes an image of some sort and at least two quotes about or by the person.

Case study

Teaching sensitive issues – slavery and Britain's role

Although it is essential that the contributions that all people make are celebrated, the darker side of history should never be ignored – prejudice, racism, inequality and for some enslavement. It is essential to know what happened in the past even if it sits uncomfortably with our national identity. The wealth of cities such as London, Liverpool and Bristol was as a result of human trafficking and the industries that profited by the slave trade helped raise the status of Britain as a trading nation and became part of the infrastructure that the Industrial Revolution was to be built upon. The slave trade stopped in 1807 but the ownership of slaves was to continue until 1833. The government gave £20 million to owners in recompense for their loss of workers, and this money was used to build or renovate some of the great houses in England. This debt was only finally paid off in 2015.

However, although children need to know the truth about the past, the way in which this is done must be age appropriate. Discussions about the conditions of the Middle Passage and the punishments inflicted are not suitable for Key Stage 2. Events could either be so sanitised that the children would not be able to engage with them at an emotional level or in an effort to make them understand, the sources used could be far too explicit. However despite these caveats it is a hugely important topic that should be discussed with upper Key Stage 2 children. In units such as the Roman Empire, early civilisations and ancient Greece, they will have discovered the use of slaves within society, and they need to recognise that this was practised in turn by Britain and other European countries in much more recent times and that slavery still exists today. This is a subject that links to human rights, citizenship and moral issues and needs to be addressed (Townsend, 2019).

One way of doing this is to show that slavery in the 18th and early 19th centuries was not something that happened somewhere else but was visible in Britain itself. Plantation owners returned to England at intervals and brought with them slaves to act as domestic servants. Slavery was not supposed to exist in England but the laws were vague and contradictory, and plantation slaves were seen legally as property and commodities that could be moved as the owner wished. There is evidence to show that many slaves fought against the system and risked severe punishment/transportation back to the colonies to escape and start a new life in Britain. Children would need some background to the transatlantic slavery, but it is important that the history is 'peopled' so that pupils can find out about individuals who had been brought to England against their will in this way. This will help them realise that this history is not abstract but is here around us. Children can also look at the physical evidence left behind which shows the wealth that was created on the back of this human suffering.

Possible activities and resources

Children need to understand what slavery is, so group work and mind maps could be a starting point for discussion. This understanding of key term is fundamental, and it is important to check for misconceptions. They also need to understand the principle of the trade triangle. This can be done using different parts of the classroom to build the triangle so that children physically walk it but without labels saying what is being traded. You could then get them to ask questions to try and understand the system and how goods and people were traded. Listening to extracts from Olaudah Equiano's autobiography should help them begin to understand the reality of this and they could link to the Human Rights Act today.

Moving the focus to Britain will help them to see the individual stories. There are some websites which show maps where graves of slaves have been recorded, for example: **http://remikapo.org/slave-graves-and-other-memorials/**. Children could use these to get information about different people and to see if they can see any patterns in distribution of the graves geographically. For more examples on how this resource could be used, refer to Townsend (2019).

There are fantastic role models against this background of human misery, such as Mary Prince, Olaudah Equiano, Ignatius Sancho and Ottobah Cugoano who were Black abolitionists. One activity could for each group to be given one name and date. They would need to find one quote, two pictures, three key facts and four reasons why they were significant. They could then write a speech which one of the group could deliver and the class could vote on the best speech.

A final activity could be for the group to make an anti-slavery memorial in whatever medium they chose – dance, mural, clay model, computer graphics or piece of music. This could encourage children to think about symbolism and the messages that they want to convey.

Case study

WW1: telling the story from different perspectives – the hidden voices

This topic could be considered as a significant event – Remembrance Day and who we remember – at Key Stage 1 or as a theme beyond 1066 at Key Stage 2. The Great War of 1914–1918 was a World War as the colonies of empires were brought into the conflict. These voices are often not heard and their sacrifices not always recognised.

Take, for example, the Indian army. When the war began in 1914, volunteers from Britain had to be recruited and trained. There was a desperate need for soldiers from the Empire, and by the end of 1914 the Indian army made up almost a third of the British Expeditionary force. By 1915, four out of the six had been moved to the Middle East where they fought against the Ottoman army in Mesopotamia. In the heat of the desert they endured a five-month siege at Kut al Amara. The city was taken and 10,000 Indian Prisoners of War were forced to march over 500 miles to Syria or even further to Anatolia. Many died and their bodies are buried in a small cemetery in Istanbul previously designated for casualties of the Crimean War. In all over 1 million Indian troops served overseas, of whom 62,000 died and another 67,000 were wounded. But there was little recognition of their feats and loyalty. Back in India where the cry for independence was growing ever louder these soldiers were seen as supporting the British oppressor, and their fight in the Middle East was forgotten by the British press who focused predominately on the Western front.

Or you could explore the contribution of the Chinese in World War One. China sent voluntary non-combatants to provide support labour, digging trenches, making munition and tank supplies. There were so many deaths and injuries that the British government reluctantly had to offer some compensation, and by the end of the war the Chinese workers were the largest and longest serving non-European contingent in World War One. Britain alone recruited 94,500. But where are their voices in the history of the war?

These are just two examples but children could find out about these events. They could research individuals whose names are on war graves and find out as much as they can about them. They can use a map of the world to find where these soldiers came from and where they were fighting. For all children it is important to ask them if they know of any of their family who was in World War One and find out about their own family history.

CHAPTER SUMMARY

History should be diverse by its very nature but the stories that are told are often from one racial perspective. The discussions around race, diversity and decolonising the curriculum are wide-ranging, and this chapter can only touch upon some of the key elements of these issues. One message should be very clear, however. In schools we need to celebrate our shared history and recognise the contributions of all across the boundaries of race, religion and geographical location. As teachers we should ensure that what we are teaching is relevant to our children and creates, rather than divides, our communities.

References

Ajegbo, K., Kuwan, D. and Sharma, S. (2007) *Curriculum Review: Diversity and Citizenship*. London: DfE.

Alexander, C., Chatterji, J. and Weekes-Bernard, D. (2012) *Making British Histories: Diversity and the National Curriculum*. London: Runnymede.

Banks, J.A. (2006) *Race, Culture and Education*. Abingdon: Routledge.

Bracey, P., Gove-Humphries, A. and Jackson, D. (2011) Teaching diversity in the history classroom. In I. Davies (ed.), *Debates in History Teaching*. London: Routledge, pp. 172–185.

Bradbury, A. (2020) A critical race theory framework for education policy analysis: the case for bilingual learners and assessment policy in England. In D. Gilborn (ed.), *Race, Ethnicity and Education 2020*, Vol. 2. London: Routledge, pp. 241–260.

Charles, E. (2019) Decolonizing the curriculum. *Insights, 32*(1): 24. **http://doi.org/10.1629/uksg.475**.

Dennis, N. (2016) *Beyond Tokenism: Teaching a Diverse History in the Post 14 Curriculum* Teaching History 165. London: Historical Association.

Department for Education National History Curriculum Key Stages 1 and 2. Available at: **https://assets.publishing.service.gov.uk/government/uploads/system/uploads/attachment_data/file/239035/PRIMARY_national_curriculum_-_History.pdf**.

Department for Education FE Commission on Race and Ethnic Disparities Report March 2020. Available at: **https://assets.publishing.service.gov.uk/government/uploads/system/uploads/attachment_data/file/974507/20210331_-_CRED_Report_-_FINAL_-_Web_Accessible.pdf**.

Harris, R. and Clarke, G. (2011) Embracing diversity in the history curriculum: a study of the challenges facing trainee teachers. *Cambridge Journal of Education, 41*(2): 159–175.

Joaquin, N. (1988) *Culture and History*. Philippines: Anvil Publishing.

Ofsted (2021) *History Review*. Available at: **https://www.gov.uk/government/publications/research-review-series-history/research-review-series-history**

Osler, A. (2009) Patriotism, multiculturalism and belonging: political discourse and the teaching of history. *Educational Review, 61*(1): 85–100.

Phillips, R. (2002) *Reflective Teaching of History*. London: Continuum, pp. 11–18.

Qualifications Curriculum Authority. (2008). *National Curriculum for History*. Norwich: QCA Publications.

The Black Curriculum. (2021) *British Black History in the National Curriculum Report 2021*. London: The Black Curriculum.

The Swann Report. (1985) *Education for All*. Report of the Committee of Enquiry into the Education of Children from Ethnic Minority Groups. London: Her Majesty's Stationery Office.

Townsend, S. (2019) *Teaching Sensitive Subjects: Slavery and Britain's Role in the Trade Primary History 83*. London: Historical Association.

4

LGBTQ+INCLUSION IN THE PRIMARY HISTORY CURRICULUM

DAMIENNE CLARKE AND GARY PYKITT

KEYWORDS: ACTUALISING; DIVERSITY; INCLUSION; INTERSECTIONALITY; LGBTQ+; REPRESENTATION; USUALISING

CHAPTER OBJECTIVES

The aims of this chapter are:

- To explore LGBTQ+ inclusion as part of a diverse and meaningful curriculum that is representative of the past.
- To provoke critical thought around the 'why?' of curriculum choices in order to consider issues around diversity as part of the primary history curriculum.
- To provide case study examples relating to LGBTQ+ individuals and events in history.

CCF ITE links

3.1	A school's curriculum enables it to set out its vision for the knowledge, skills and values that its pupils will learn, within a coherent wider vision for successful learning.
3.2	Secure subject knowledge helps teachers to motivate pupils and teach effectively.

(Continued)

(Continued)

3.7	In all subject areas, pupils learn new ideas by linking those ideas to existing knowledge, organising this knowledge into increasingly complex mental models (or 'schemata'); carefully sequencing teaching to facilitate this process is important.
4.2	Effective teachers introduce new material in steps, explicitly linking new ideas to what has been previously studied and learned.
4.3	Modelling helps pupils understand new processes and ideas; good models make abstract ideas concrete and accessible.

Introduction

While the National Curriculum (2013a) sets out the minimum expectations for children's entitlement, as teachers we need to be aware of a much wider range of factors to ensure we are delivering a curriculum which captures the complexity and richness of society. In terms of the primary history of National Curriculum, this is made explicit within its 'Purpose of Study':

> *History helps pupils to understand the complexity of people's lives, the process of change, the diversity of societies and relationships between different groups, as well as their own identity and the challenges of their time.*

> (DfE, 2013b: 1)

This chapter explores how developing an LGBTQ+ inclusive history curriculum not only supports schools in fulfilling their wider statutory and moral duties, but also supports primary pupils in developing a secure history knowledge and understanding.

We will consider the importance of the choices we make when planning for children's learning and how small, but considered, changes to curricular provision can have a big impact.

REFLECTION

Think about your own experiences as a learner:

- Which different identities were visible in the curriculum and how?
- Did you feel the curriculum was relevant and representative of you and your peers?
- To what extent were LGBTQ+ histories and stories included within your curriculum?
- Did teaching make assumptions?

LGBT+ inclusion

- What do we mean by LGBTQ+ inclusion within the curriculum?
- Why does LGBTQ+ inclusion matter?
- What are schools' statutory duties?
- Why is a whole-school approach important?

The acronym LGBTQ+, when used in the context of the curriculum, particularly in primary schools can be a source of contention. This contention is frequently seen in the media and is often due to misconceptions and preconceptions of what LGBTQ+ inclusive education looks like, usually focused on issues concerning sex. Ofsted (2021a) research notes the importance of effective communication with parents/carers to enable understanding of what will be taught and why. This information can be presented in a range of ways to ensure that the curriculum and school values related to the teaching of the protected characteristics is made clear to eliminate the potential for misinformation.

The DFE (2019) statutory guidance on Relationships Education for primary pupils is a positive starting point for professional discussions. The emphasis being on relationships and the diverse forms relationships may take with a focus on social justice related to all of the protected characteristics as defined in the Equality Act 2010.

Ofsted (2021b) emphasises addressing LGBTQ+ issues in age-appropriate ways with a particular focus on 'the different types of family groups that exist within society'. We live in a diverse world and children are an active part of this world. An LGBTQ+ inclusive curriculum needs to ensure that all identities are visible, recognised and celebrated throughout the curriculum. Gates and Buckler (2020) note the importance of ensuring that children engage with a curriculum that is diverse and representative, as without this, children may seek information from unreliable sources without support.

The Equality Act 2010 is centred on respect for the full range of protected characteristics, including sex, sexual orientation and gender reassignment. The Act underpins the legal duties on teachers to ensure that all protected characteristics are represented throughout the curriculum in a positive way.

Todd (2018: 93) notes that under the Equality Act 2010 and Public Sector Equality Duty, schools '... have to go beyond non-discrimination and be proactive in advancing equality'.

History is made up of stories, events and characters representative of the full range of protected characteristics, but how often do we, as teachers, shy away from topics or individuals that may be perceived as more difficult or contentious? Charlesworth (2015: 66) notes that, 'Silence can send the loudest message about the value placed on lesbian, gay and bisexual identities'. With historic, but impactful legislation such as Section 28, which prohibited the promotion of homosexuality from 1988 to 2003, it is understandable that teachers may feel anxious about LGBTQ+ inclusion. Ofsted (2021a) research raises schools' concerns around the clarity within the current curriculum guidance that impedes confidence and understanding around the requirements.

Barnes and Carlile (2018: 134) highlight the notion of usualising; '…a teaching pedagogy that makes the range of people's characteristics something people come into contact with on an everyday basis, thus making them so usual as not to become taboo, or subject to ridicule or bullying'. Seen in this way, it is clear that a whole-school approach, and a carefully structured long-term plan, is needed to ensure fair and equitable representation of the full range of protected characteristics meaningfully embedded in the school's ethos through routine practice. Ofsted (2021b) notes that it is not necessary to teach about all of the protected characteristics in every year group, but emphasise that fair and equitable coverage of the range should be evident to support children's developing knowledge and understanding. An audit of your existing planning is a helpful starting point.

The Equality Act is integral to Ofsted inspections and is inherent in the language of the *Education Inspection Framework* (Ofsted, 2021c) and *Inspecting the teaching of the protected characteristics in schools* (Ofsted, 2021b). They note that LGBTQ+ issues should not be addressed as isolated lessons, but should be 'integrated appropriately into the curriculum' (Ofsted, 2021b). There is a clear expectation that children's appreciation of all of the protected characteristics should be fostered effectively and failure to do so has the potential to lead to lower Ofsted gradings:

> If inspectors identify at inspection that a school is not teaching about all the protected characteristics, they will always report on this and will explain how (if at all) it has affected the school's inspection judgements.
>
> (Ofsted, 2021b)

While there is clearly a legal dimension to this issue, Ofsted's (2021a) research about the teaching of sex, sexual orientation and gender reassignment highlights the **moral** rather than legal underpinning, for schools' creation of a culture of mutual respect across the protected characteristics. Effective and meaningful inclusion of LGBTQ+ identities enhances personal, social and emotional outcomes for children and helps to prepare them for the diverse modern world. History as a subject is one example given in the study, 'In many primary schools in the sample, pupils were introduced to LGBT role models, such as historical or present influential LGBT people' (Ofsted, 2021a).

It is important to note that, at primary level, children should be introduced to concepts, and the range of characteristics should be usualised to give them secure foundations for future learning when they will become familiar with the finer details associated with the issues.

Why is LGBTQ+ inclusion in the curriculum important?

> How does an LGBTQ+ inclusive curriculum enable schools to meet National Curriculum requirements for primary history?

Style (1988) uses the metaphor of the curriculum as both a window and mirror to argue the importance of a diverse curriculum and critically analyse the limitations of one which is non-diverse. The mirror is when pupils see themselves in the curriculum, i.e. the curriculum reflects aspects of themselves and their experiences and identities, thereby representing them within the curriculum which both validates and values them. With the curriculum as a window, the idea of looking through it and being introduced to, and exploring the lives and experiences of individuals who possess different identities and who have had different experiences is presented. When the curriculum has a balance of both window and mirror, then pupils are supported in understanding and celebrating diversity and their place in the world.

When considered in relation to LGBTQ+ primary history, this benefits all pupils. Ensuring the place of LGBTQ+ history within the curriculum values and validates the experiences of LGBTQ+ people in history and by that 'mirror reflection', LGBTQ+ pupils themselves. At the same time, it fosters knowledge, understanding and respect among all pupils. Thus the importance of the choices we make when planning and subsequently teaching our LGBTQ+ inclusive history curriculum cannot be underestimated:

> The decisions we make about what is available to students are the curriculum. If we aren't being thoughtful about the materials, we aren't designing the curriculum, and if we aren't challenging stereotypes, we are perpetuating them.

> (Rycroft-Smith and Andre, 2020: 84–85)

Ensuring an LGBTQ+ inclusive history curriculum better reflects history itself. Irrespective of whether LGBTQ+ stories have been included and acknowledged within schools' curricula, they exist, they are there and they are an important part of history.

> History is filled with lesbian, gay, bisexual and transgender people. We know this through rare published histories, court transcripts, and other sources. For years, much of this history was hidden, ignored, or erased by those who would rather not discuss it. But it is a fascinating, rich history, and our world would not be the same without the contributions of the LGBT community, invisible or not.

> (Pohlen, 2016: 3)

Decisions about where to include LGBTQ+ history within the primary history curriculum will take place on different levels and should be part of the discussion around structuring the wider history curriculum across the primary age phases. To avoid being tokenistic, LGBTQ+ history should be embedded within the larger context of the school's curriculum in terms of developing knowledge, skills and understanding and shouldn't, for example, only appear once a year during LGBTQ+ History Month. Teachers have opportunity to include and explore LGBTQ+ histories within their day-to-day teaching.

The *History Research Review* (2021d) identifies that pupils' progress depends on the 'range and depth of their existing knowledge and how secure it is in their minds' at each stage of their learning and highlights the importance of learning through 'meaningful examples and repeated encounters'. Careful considering of *what, where* and *how* LGBTQ+ histories are included and taught within the curriculum can secure well-developed and rich subject knowledge and understanding over time.

For schools who have already planned their history curriculum but want to develop it to be more LGBTQ+ inclusive, small but considered changes can have a big impact:

- When choosing significant individuals to teach in Key Stage 1, do your chosen individuals include LGBTQ+ representation?

- If planning a themed topic in Key Stage 2, is there opportunity to develop this further to meaningfully include aspects of LGBTQ+ history?

It is important to note, however, that this is not about shoehorning something into tick a box; choices made should be of genuine value to children's history learning.

Transgender history

Trans: short for 'transgender'. The term used to describe a person who identifies as a different gender to the one they were assigned at birth.

(Barnes and Carlile, 2018: 133)

Understanding of diverse gender identities has evolved over a number of years, as has the language related to it. However, there is still a level of uncertainty among many over its usage and meaning.

Morgan and Taylor (2019), cited by Hamilton (2021), note how this could be due to the notions of 'childhood "innocence" and the protection of a "natural" state of cisgenderedness' (p. 136) – 'cisgender' being the term used to describe a person 'whose gender identity is the same as the sex they were assigned at birth' (Stonewall, 2019: 39). Language is complex, nuanced and individual and continues to evolve. Gender manifests itself in a range of ways and does not always correlate to cisgenderedness.

Issues around gender variance are becoming more widely represented. However, this is still an area of history which needs much further exploration and exposition.

In terms of developing an LGBTQ+ inclusive primary history curriculum, this means making conscious choices to include transgender stories. These are not always easy to identify as in many (although not all) societies and cultures in history; LGBTQ+ issues, which include trans issues, were not discussed, or if they were, they were often spoken about negatively (Pohlen, 2016). However, trans stories are there and continue to emerge, and it is important that we include them within our curricular provision.

Pedagogical approaches

While our choices of subject content are important, so too is *how* this content will be included and taught. In terms of history teaching and learning in general, this is no different than with any other history topic but in terms of LGBTQ+ histories there are particular pedagogies that are useful to adopt.

'Usualising' and 'actualising' are teaching approaches used by Schools OUT (2021) across all curriculum subjects to promote equal rights and respect for LGBTQ+ people and challenge discrimination and prejudice.

These approaches are an effective way to include LGBTQ+ history within the primary curriculum in a meaningful way and to secure children's historical knowledge and understanding over time.

Usualising

Earlier in this chapter, the pedagogical approach of 'usualising' was introduced as a way to include LGBTQ+ history within the primary curriculum, rather than specifically remarking upon, or considering LGBTQ+ issues or a person's identity or sexuality.

Usualising is described by Sanders (2009) as the 'innate inclusion of LGBTQ stories and experiences within our everyday talk and teaching' and as such is a referential method of teaching rather than instructional. This approach is suitable for use throughout the primary history curriculum.

> *Usualising LGBT lives means that learners are made aware of the diversity of LGBT people, that they are found in every culture, near and far, and that they share many characteristics with people who are heterosexual.*
>
> *It is also about acknowledging the differences between LGBT individuals themselves that they do not all conform to the same behaviours/appearance.*
>
> (The Classroom, 2021b)

The quote, while not directly referring to the history curriculum, can nonetheless be applied to it and reminds us that not only do we need to ensure we have a balance of LGBTQ+ historical figures and histories within our curriculum, we also need to represent other aspects of diversity within the LGBTQ+ histories as well, for example, ethnicity or disability. This overlap of identities and personal characteristics is known as 'intersectionality' (Crenshaw, 2019) and recognises that individuals often have more than one aspect of their identity that is subject to discrimination and prejudice.

> Note, the term 'usualise' as opposed to 'normalise'. 'Normalise' is problematic when applied to people as it can suggest that there is a 'right' way to be. This can be seen as 'pejorative' by many people who may consider themselves 'outside the majority' and as such does not embrace diversity in the way in which we are aiming for (The Classroom, 2021).

Actualising

Through usualising, pupils become aware of different LGBTQ+ individuals in history. This lays the foundations for exploring LGBTQ+ lives, histories and issues in greater depth at a later stage. In this way, actualising builds upon usualising. An important point made by Schools OUT (2021) is that the actualising teaching approach should not be taken unless the focus in question has previously been usualised. When children are accustomed to learning about LGBTQ+ lives, then they have a basis for developing learning further with learning objectives relating specifically to LGBTQ+ history. An example of how this might be done is presented later in the chapter.

Broadly speaking, and suggested by Schools OUT (2021), while usualising should be part of our whole primary curriculum from Early Years Foundation Stage (EYFS) upwards, the actualising approach will be more commonly adopted in Key Stage 2 or above.

Effective use of actualising in history teaching and learning supports pupils in developing understanding of 'the complexity of people's lives, the process of change, the diversity of societies and relationships between different groups, as well as their own identity and the challenges of their time' (DfE, 2013).

A primary history curriculum, which is LGBTQ+ inclusive, will include LGBTQ+ people and issues within its chosen topics, whether that is by reference (usualising) or for specific consideration (actualising).

Case study

Key Stage 1: Significant Individuals – challenging gender stereotypes and standing up to prejudice and discrimination while also being a positive LGBTQ+ role model.

This example of practice focuses on Lily Parr (1905–1978) and could be developed into a unit of work for children in Key Stage 1. It meets the primary history National Curriculum requirement for children to learn about *'the lives of significant individuals in the past who have contributed to national and international achievements'* (DfE, 2013: 2).

This example assumes that children have already learnt about other significant individuals and therefore have a developing understanding of the concept of *'significance'*.

Lily Parr (1905–1978)

Lily Parr was born in St Helen's into a poor family where she was one of seven children. Lily refused to conform to gender stereotypes and, rather than cooking or sewing, preferred to play football and rugby.

When World War One broke out and men left their jobs to fight, women took on their roles, including working in factories. Women's factory football teams were formed and were considered to be a good way to keep the women workers healthy and boost morale.

Lily's footballing talent was spotted by the manager of the Dick, Kerr Ladies Team (which represented a factory in Preston), and Lily went to work at the factory and joined the team where she was very successful.

However, in 1921 the English FA banned women from playing at their venues and Lily's dream of being a professional footballer was over.

That didn't stop Lily and her team mates from playing football though, and Lily fought against prejudice and adversity to keep women's football going. Lily also qualified as a nurse and lived with her partner Mary. They were happy together and very open about their relationship despite the discrimination they faced at the time. Lily and Mary bought a house together – making Lily the first person in her family to own one.

Lily was the first woman to be inducted into the National Football Museum's Hall of Fame in 2002, and in 2019 she became the first female footballer to be commemorated with a statue.

In 1971, the Football Association finally lifted its ban on women's teams playing in their venues.

Lily Parr is hugely significant; as well as being a pioneer of women's football, she is also an LGBTQ+ icon and role model (Table 4.1).

Table 4.1   Activity ideas

Exploring children's perceptions		
It is important to explore children's current perceptions and the understanding that they begin the learning with. For example, children might not realise that women's football is not a recent thing.	What does a footballer look like?	Draw a footballer (keep children's images to revisit at the end of the taught unit)
	Which footballers do you know? How do you know about them? Where have you heard about them?	Develop understanding of how we know and that we know about individual who we have evidence of – doesn't mean that there aren't others we don't know about.
	Compile list/pictures of those children have identified – any observations?	Be open to any observations children may make.
Who was Lily Parr and why is she significant?		
Share a photograph of Lily Parr – model enquiry approaches.	Describe what you see. What do you think this photograph might tell us about Lily Parr? Why do you think that? How sure can we be? What doesn't the photograph tell us? What questions would you like to ask Lily?	
Looking at more evidence This works well when children are placed in small groups, enabling discussion and collaboration. Teaching can be adapted accordingly, for example, through adult support, using stem sentences or introducing images at a pace to suit children's learning.	Using a selection of visual images, engage children in evidence handling and enquiry. Encourage children to form hypotheses about Lily's life and sequence the images they have in a possible chronological order, giving reasons for their choices. Once completed, children can go on a 'timeline tour' and see how other groups have sequenced the images and the reason for their choices? Does it make them think about their own choices? Do they want to make any changes? If so, why?	
The story of Lily Parr's life		
There is a lot of information about Lily Parr's life which can be found online. There are also children's story books which can be used to support storytelling, e.g. Trailblazer by Elizabeth Dale.	Tell the story of Lily's life to provide the children with an overview narrative of it. Encourage children to reflect on the interpretations they made from the evidence they had. Did they have enough evidence to make accurate decisions? Do they need to make any changes? What can they add to their sequenced timeline of Lily's life after hearing her story? Check children's understanding and address any inaccuracies in their sequenced timelines.	
Timelines and maps		
Add Lily Parr's birth/death dates to it to a whole-school timeline. What else was happening at the time Lily was alive? What other significant individuals/events have children have already learnt about? Where are they placed chronologically in relation to Lily? Etc. Children have already begun to construct timelines of Lily's life and related key events – these can be developed further over the course of learning about Lily and a scaled timeline of Lily's life could be constructed.		

(Continued)

Table 4.1   (Continued)

Exploring children's perceptions
Use maps to locate key places in Lily's life: Where was Lily born? Where did she move to when she play for the Dick, Kerr Ladies Team? Where did she travel to play football? Where did she and Mary buy their house?

Developing learning in depth	
The learning activities enable children to gain a good overview of Lily's life from which they can explore aspects in more depth and ensure a rich historical context for learning.	Example lesson enquiry focuses: • What was Lily's childhood like? Why was Lily considered to be different from many other girls? • How did Lily become a footballer? • What was Lily's life like when she played for the Dick, Kerr Ladies Team? • Why couldn't Lily play football professionally? Was this fair? What did Lily do when she found this out? • How did Lily's life as a footballer compare with a contemporary successful English female footballer (for example, Casey Stoney who is a former professional footballer, manager and current head coach of an international team)? • What impact did the FA ban in 1921 have on women's professional football? How might things have been different if the ban had not been made? • Why was Lily Parr the first female footballer to be commemorated with a statue? Why should we remember her?

Children could revisit the pictures they drew at the start of the learning and, through teacher questioning be supported to reflect on any change in their perceptions and consider wider questions about equity, discrimination and gender stereotypes.

Rooting learning within a strong historical context supports children to not only develop their substantive knowledge and understanding of the past but also provides a meaningful focus through which disciplinary knowledge and methods of enquiry can be developed.

There are strong and natural links which could be made to physical education (PE), giving children of all genders opportunity to play football and develop their skills in this area.

Developing the curriculum

Early Years and Foundation Stage: using stories

> *We are not 'born' with a gender, in the sense that we are not born with the constraints and expectations of gender roles that later may come to define us.*
>
> (Rycroft-Smith and Andre, 2020: 171)

Stories are an important part of young children's way of making sense of and understanding their world (Temple, 2016). Using stories in the EYFS can develop children's early history skills and understanding and also provide opportunities for children to distinguish between fact and fiction. Stories also present an opportunity to challenge stereotypical attitudes and assumptions.

Gender stereotypes are still very present in society and have the potential to impose barriers and limits on children's aspirations and life choices. Working with stories that challenge outdated gender stereotypes can support children in developing a confident sense of self and the ability to question gender stereotypes they may encounter.

Stories can also be used to develop understanding of, and respect for, the similarities and differences that exist between people.

Examples could include:

- *Ada Twist, Scientist* by Andrea Beaty

- *Mary Wears What She Wants* by Keith Negley

- *Made by Raffi* by Craig Pomranz

- *Clive and His Babies* by Jessica Spanyol

- *William's Doll* by Charlotte Zolotow

Key Stage 1: Usualising – suggestions for teaching

The following LGBTQ+ individuals have 'contributed to national and international achievements' in different ways and are examples of significant individuals who could be meaningfully included within the Key Stage 1 history curriculum:

- Nicola Adams (born 1982): first female boxer to become Olympic champion

- Frida Kahlo (1907–1954): one of Mexico's greatest artists

- Sally Ride (1951–2012): astronaut, physicist and first American woman in space

- Bayard Rustin (1912–1987): advisor to Martin Luther King and peaceful civil rights activist

- We'wha (1849–1896): Zuni Native American Pueblo leader and Lhamana (meaning Two-Spirit)

- Emma Wiggs MBE (born 1980): double Paralympic gold medal winner and nine times World Champion paracanoeist

You can read more about some of these individuals, and many others, in *'Rainbow Revolutionaries'* by Sarah Prager.

Key Stage 2: Actualising – suggestions for teaching

An area of history still commonly taught in many schools, often as part of a 'study of an aspect or theme of British history that extends pupils' chronological knowledge', is World War Two (WW2). Within this, a study of Alan Turing and his role in breaking enemy codes is a popular focus and is also a well-resourced area of history.

Alan Turing's story also provides meaningful opportunity for an **actualising** approach to be taken with older children. This can enable them to develop greater understanding of Alan Turing and what aspects of life were like in Britain at the time he lived. Alan Turing was gay and lived at a time when homosexuality was illegal. In 1952, Alan Turing was convicted for 'gross indecency' because he had a homosexual relationship.

Children can explore both this aspect of Alan Turing's history and the wider historical context, with its many complex issues that surrounded it, including legalised discrimination and prejudice, changing attitudes over time and the people who have fought against this kind of discrimination and prejudice in order to gain equal rights for LGBTQ+ people.

Alan Turing's contribution was not known about for many years but he has gone from being a hidden figure to a much celebrated public figure. Alan Turing was posthumously pardoned in 2013, and in 2017, a law, informally known as 'Alan Turing's Law' posthumously pardoned approximately 50,000 gay and bisexual men who had also been convicted of offences which have since been abolished.

Consideration of the contributions of other members of the LGBTQ+ community in WW2 could also be made, for example, Roberta Cowell. Roberta Cowell was a transgender pioneer, who as well as being a successful racing driver was also an RAF Spitfire pilot in WW2. She was captured by German forces and held prisoner of war until 1945 when the camp she was held in was liberated by the Red Army.

Alan Turing and Roberta Cowell not only made significant contribution to Britain's war effort, but both have played an important role in making LGBTQ+ identities more visible and overcoming discrimination and prejudice through their legacies and lives.

REFLECTION

Using the case study and suggestions for teaching as a starting point, identify key areas for your own development in relation to:

- Subject content knowledge
- Disciplinary knowledge and understanding

REFLECTION

What are the implications for your future practice in terms of:

- Curriculum choices made?
- How you could challenge stereotypes through your teaching?
- How to ensure that children develop their historical knowledge, skills and understanding through an inclusive curriculum?

┌─────────────── **CHAPTER SUMMARY** ───────────────┐

This chapter aims to support primary teachers as they develop their LGBTQ+ inclusive history curriculum. We hope that it will provide a starting point for teachers to reflect on what they already do and to continue to develop their subject knowledge and curricular provision with increased confidence.

The past is diverse and is woven from many different narratives and experiences. As such, it is important that this is represented within our curricular provision and that children are enabled to view history through a diverse range of individuals, groups and experiences. LGBTQ+ histories are becoming more widely represented, with more stories being revealed over time. Embedding these within our primary history curriculum can only enrich children's knowledge and understanding of the past.

└───┘

References

Barnes, E. and Carlile, A. (2018) *How to Transform Your School Into an LGBT+ Friendly Place*. London: Jessica Kingsley Publishers.

Charlesworth, J. (2015) *That's So Gay!*. London: Jessica Kingsley Publishers.

Crenshaw, K. (2019) *On Intersectionality: The Essential Writings of Kimberlé Crenshaw*. New York, NY: The New Press.

Department for Education (2013a) *National Curriculum*. Available at: **https://www.gov.uk/government/collections/national-curriculum** (accessed 17 December 2021)

Department for Education (2013b) *The National Curriculum in England: History Programmes of Study – Key Stages 1 and 2*. Available at: **https://assets.publishing.service.gov.uk/government/uploads/system/uploads/attachment_data/file/239035/PRIMARY_national_curriculum_-_History.pdf** (accessed 17 December 2021)

Department for Education (2019) *Relationships Education, Relationships and Sex Education (RSE) and Health Education*. Available at: **https://www.gov.uk/government/publications/relationships-education-relationships-and-sex-education-rse-and-health-education** (accessed 17 December 2021)

Gates, J. and Buckler, S. (2020) *Lessons in Love and Understanding: Relationships, Sexuality and Gender in the Classroom*. London: Corwin.

Hamilton, P. (2021) *Diversity and Marginalisation in Childhood*. London: SAGE.

Stonewall (2019) *List of LGBTQ+ Terms*. Available at: **https://www.stonewall.org.uk/help-advice/faqs-and-glossary/list-lgbtq-terms**.

Ofsted (2021a) *Research Commentary: Teaching About Sex, Sexual Orientation and Gender Reassignment.* Available at: **https://www.gov.uk/government/speeches/research-commentary-teaching-about-sex-sexual-orientation-and-gender-reassignment** (accessed 17 December 2021)

Ofsted (2021b) *Inspecting Teaching of the Protected Characteristics in Schools.* Available at: **https://www.gov.uk/government/publications/inspecting-teaching-of-the-protected-characteristics-in-schools/inspecting-teaching-of-the-protected-characteristics-in-schools** (accessed 17 December 2021)

Ofsted (2021c) *Education Inspection Framework.* Available at: **https://www.gov.uk/government/publications/education-inspection-framework** (accessed 17 December 2021)

Ofsted (2021d) *Research Review Series: History.* Available at: **https://www.gov.uk/government/publications/research-review-series-history** (accessed 17 December 2021)

Pohlen, J. (2016) *Gay and Lesbian History for Kids.* Chicago, IL: Chicago Review Press.

Prager, S. (2020) *Rainbow Revolutionaries.* New York, NY: Harper Collins.

Rycroft-Smith, L. and Andre, G. (2020) *The Equal Classroom.* Abingdon: Routledge.

Sanders, S. (2009) Verbalising and Usualising the LGBTQ+ Community TEDX GoodenoughCollege Video. **https://www.youtube.com/watch?v=QfY4AZLvx4M.**

Schools OUT (2021) Available at: **http://www.schools-out.org.uk/** (accessed 17 December 2021)

Style, E. (1988) Curriculum as Window and Mirror *Social Science Record*, Fall, 1996. First published in *Listening for All Voices*. Summit, NJ: Oak Knoll School Monograph.

Temple, S. (Summer 2016) Time for a story: using stories in the Early Years and Foundation Stage. *Primary History*, *73*: 10–11.

The Classroom (2021a) Available at: **http://the-classroom.org.uk/** (accessed 17 December 2021)

The Classroom (2021b) *'Usualising' and 'Actualising'.* Available at: **http://the-classroom.org.uk/how-to-do-it/usualising-and-actualising/** (accessed 17 December 2021)

Todd, M. (2018) *Straight Jacket: Overcoming Society's Legacy of Gay Shame.* London: Black Swan.

5

THE POWER OF A LANGUAGE-AWARE CURRICULUM IN MULTILINGUAL CLASSROOMS

MOIRA BRAZIL

KEYWORDS: ACTIVE BILINGUALISM; COMMON UNDERLYING PROFICIENCY (CUP); FUNDS OF KNOWLEDGE; INTERSECTIONALITY; MONOLINGUAL MINDSET; SUPERDIVERSITY; TRANSLANGUAGING

CHAPTER OBJECTIVES

The aims of this chapter are:

- To consider the linguistic complexity of England's 'superdiverse' pupil population.
- To examine some key concepts in additional language acquisition theory and the importance of children's 'home' languages in supporting and enhancing learning.
- To consider some approaches to enhancing linguistic awareness across the curriculum.

CCF ITE links

1.3	Teacher expectations can affect pupil outcomes and setting goals that challenge and stretch pupils is essential.
1.5	A culture of mutual trust and respect supports effective relationships.
3.1	A school's curriculum enables it to set out its vision for the knowledge, skills and values that its pupils will learn, encompassing the national curriculum within a coherent wider vision for successful learning.
3.7	Pupils learn new ideas [concepts in English as an additional language (EAL)] by linking those ideas to existing knowledge [concepts in home language(s)].
5.2	Seeking to understand pupils' differences, including their different levels of prior knowledge and potential barriers to learning, is an essential part of teaching.
8.4	Building effective relationships with parents, carers and families can improve pupils' motivation, behaviour and academic success.
8.7	Engaging in high-quality professional development can help teachers improve.

Although no specific mention is made of the EAL pupil group in the Core Curriculum Framework (CCF), The Bell Foundation (2020) has mapped relevant EAL content across the Teachers Standards; this chapter will draw on that guidance.

Introduction

The number of multilingual pupils in primary schools has risen steadily in recent years, yet research suggests newly qualified teachers in England are unsure how best to meet these learners' needs (DfE, 2018; Foley et al., 2018). Current government guidance on EAL is minimal and multilingual learners are arguably positioned in deficit within the current primary National Curriculum (NC), where scant attention is paid to the linguistic and cultural knowledge these pupils have which might both support their learning and enhance that of others.

This chapter proposes an alternative view, in which multilingual pupils' linguistic and cultural funds of knowledge (Gonzalez et al., 2005) are used to move beyond a monolingual mindset in policy and practice (Conteh, 2019) towards a more 'language-aware' curriculum which reflects England's linguistic diversity and enhances learning and inclusion. Concepts in additional language acquisition and cultural theory will be explored in relation to a case study school and practical examples offered of ways to make the most of children's language repertoires. This is particularly important in the current post-Brexit context and wider political discourses that are impacting upon school communities (Anderson et al., 2016). This chapter will argue teachers' sociolinguistic consciousness and disposition towards advocacy for multilingual learners (Lucas and Villegas, 2011) is the best way forward towards meeting the needs of our super-diverse pupil population.

Who are these pupils?

Although currently comprising 20.9% of the pupil population (DfE, 2021), the distribution of EAL learners varies widely across England, from schools with a multilingual majority to others in which a single, newly arrived EAL learner may be the first encountered by some staff. Conteh (2019) considers EAL an 'umbrella' term, as it refers to a wide range of pupils with differing experiences of formal schooling and levels of confidence in English. Many multilingual learners are UK nationals from settled communities while others may have arrived directly from abroad due to very differing reasons including voluntary or forced migration. Recognising the extent of England's **superdiversity** (Vertovec, 2007) is important, as multilingual learners with EAL will have different starting points in terms of their journey into learning English through the Early Years Foundation Stage (EYFS) Framework and NC. Some learners will be fully fluent in English and completely integrated into the school and wider community, whereas others will be new to the language and culture of the United Kingdom and may face significant social and economic exclusion.

As with any pupil, there are many factors which may impact on an individual EAL learner's presentation in school. It is especially important to clarify that developing English as an additional language is not the same as having a Special Educational Need; that said, some multilingual pupils may also have a Special Educational Need (SEN). The heterogenous nature this pupil group is recognised in the current NC 'Inclusion' section:

> Teachers must also take account of the needs of pupils whose first language is not English. Monitoring of progress should take account of the pupil's age, length of time in this country, previous educational experience and ability in other languages.

(DfE, 2013: 8)

Currently the Department for Education does not require schools to collect data on EAL pupils' Proficiency in English (PIE). This is concerning as research suggests that PIE is the single most important factor impacting pupils' achievement (Strand and Lindorff, 2020). Having English as an additional language is not a barrier to high achievement, and we will see how it can enhance cognition and learning. Understanding the profile of achievement of EAL pupils is arguably more complex than may appear in government data (DfE, 2019), particularly when considering those pupils who may be at risk of underachievement. Jim Cummins' (2018) research on linguistic minority pupils across several countries suggests potential underachievement may be the result of a number of different factors (Figure 5.1):

- home language (L1) and school language (L2/English) are different

- low family income and/or low levels of parental education

- pupils' group/community are subject to social discrimination or racism in the wider society

While all pupils with EAL must move from their 'home' language (L1) to English (L2) to access the curriculum, the concept of **intersectionality** helps explain the potentially different positions of learners, as some pupils may face one or both additional factors. That said, although these challenges are viewed as potential underachievement 'risk' factors, Cummins notes they '...become realised as actual educational disadvantage only when the school fails to respond appropriately or reinforces the negative impact of the broader social factors' (2018: 68). From this we recognise all EAL learners have an entitlement to an engaging and effective curricular offer; however, particular attention should be paid to those multilingual pupils who may face additional challenges.

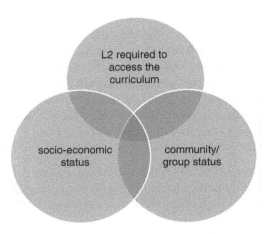

Figure 5.1   Factors impacting pupils (Source: *Adapted from Cummins, 2018*).

REFLECTION

Think of a child....

Find out whether there is a child in your class, key phase or wider school who has one or more languages in addition to English in their repertoire. Schools complete an annual Census which includes a 'First language' question: 'A pupil is recorded to have English as an additional language if they are exposed to a language at home that is known or believed to be other than English. This measure is not a measure of English language proficiency or a good proxy for recent immigration' (DfE, 2021).

Ask your mentor to help you discover more about this learner; the suggestions below will help you begin to explore some of their complexities:

- length of time in English-medium schooling
- prior schooling or literacy (in the United Kingdom and/or abroad, in any of their languages)
- if they are eligible for Pupil Premium or Free School Meals
- any identified additional needs (e.g. SEND); information from parents on presentation outside school

---

What is the current DfE policy on EAL and how do schools cater for the needs of multilingual learners?

Schools vary considerably in terms of EAL provision; your school or setting may have well-established policy, named staff with responsibility for EAL and Continuing Professional Development (CPD) training opportunities. Conversely there may be no policy or mention of EAL or multilingualism in your school or setting. Whatever your context, knowing more about multilingualism can help develop a 'language-aware' approach to the curriculum that will support and enhance the teaching and learning offered to these pupils.

As EAL learners are immersed in English in the mainstream classroom, there is an expectation they will 'pick up' English naturally; this is implied in the current NC, which states:

> 4.6 The ability of pupils for whom English is an additional language to take part in the national curriculum may be in advance of their communication skills in English. Teachers should plan teaching opportunities to help pupils develop their English and should aim to provide the support pupils need to take part in all subjects.

> (DfE, 2013: 8)

EAL learners must therefore learn the subject content through their additional language English. While children 'immersed' in mainstream schooling will gain social fluency relatively quickly, research suggests it can take longer to become fully proficient in the academic language required to achieve within the curriculum (Conteh, 2019; Strand and Lindorff, 2020).

Looking critically at the NC, no mention is made of pupils maintaining their home language to support and enhance their learning once they can access ('take part in') curricular subjects. Unlike the NC, the EYFS guidance mentions use of children's home languages in learning:

> 1.7. For children whose home language is not English, providers must take reasonable steps to provide opportunities for children to develop and use their home language in play and learning, supporting their language development at home. Providers must also ensure that children have sufficient opportunities to learn and reach a good standard in English language during the EYFS.

> (DfE, 2017: 9)

While recognition of the importance of children's home languages is helpful, as with the absence of PIE data there are concerns regarding the 'Baseline' Reception assessment, which is conducted only in English, as this potentially disadvantages bilingual children at the outset of their educational journey (Bradbury, 2020). The term **monolingual mindset** (Conteh, 2019) could be used to critique this lack of policy recognition of bilingual learners' specific needs and an assessment system predicated on 'native' English speakers.

Despite the word 'additional' in 'EAL', some critics (Conteh, 2019; Costley and Leung, 2020) consider the current NC model results in 'transitional bilingualism', whereby English will eventually become pupils' dominant language, often at the expense of their first language. It is important to examine how language acquisition research informs an alternative model of **active bilingualism**, in which English is added to pupils' language repertoires while the continued development of home language is supported and encouraged. Cummins (2017) suggests **active bilingualism** best captures the language learning processes that multilingual learners undergo which will enhance their learning and wellbeing.

REFLECTION

Finding out about multilingualism in my class/school

Ask your mentor:

- How many pupils have a language other than English in my class? In my school/setting? How many languages are represented?
- Is there a policy that mentions EAL, multilingualism or language diversity?
- Does the school/setting provide any CPD or training on multilingual learners with EAL?
- Are there any staff with specific responsibility for multilingual learners with EAL?

How do multilingual pupils with EAL learn? What supports their academic progress and social well-being?

Research on sequential childhood bilingualism helps us better understand the processes bilingual pupils undergo as they acquire EAL, suggesting they pass through four 'stages' when moving from home language (L1) into the English language (L2) environment (Conteh, 2019):

Figure 5.2: (four stages relationship chart) Sequential process of additional language acquisition

- continuing to communicate in L1 (age dependent – younger children more typically pass through this stage)
- a 'silent period' (a potentially misleading term, as children actively listen and privately 'rehearse' L2)
- first 'public' attempts at productive speaking; characterised by repeating formulaic phrases and commonly heard words
- gaining confidence – trying out longer, more complex and creative combinations of phrases

Recognising and acknowledging multilingual learners' strengths and areas of challenge is fundamental to assessment for learning. Schools are no longer required to collect PIE data; however, some schools continue to use the PIE scale from the former 2016–2018 census to assess pupil progress against five stages from 'New to English' through 'Fully fluent' (Bell Foundation, 2019). This provides important additional data on EAL pupil progress and attainment.

Figure 5.2   Progression in a new language (please redraw)

Perhaps the least well-understood aspect of additional language acquisition is the relationship between L1 and L2, in other words how children's home language (L1) interacts with and impacts on their developing English (L2). While length of time in English-medium education is a key factor in relation to eventual attainment, research also shows pupils' academic achievement in English is enhanced by drawing on their home language. Cummins' **Common Underlying Proficiency** theory of linguistic interdependence explains how an individual's different languages are not stored in separate parts of the brain, but rather are constantly active in a dynamic and continual transfer of conceptual and linguistic skills and knowledge. Therefore, perhaps counter-intuitively, strong support for first language is associated with higher achievement in the additional language (Cummins, 2018). This is associated with the model of active bilingualism mentioned earlier, as well as the concept of **translanguaging,** which highlights how learners draw on their full language repertoire to make choices and find the most effective way to achieve their communicative goals. This 'switching' between languages is not a result of confusion, but rather a purposeful and creative use of language to best meet the communicative demands of a given context, and often occurs sub-consciously (Conteh, 2019).

It is therefore important pupils with EAL receive encouragement and opportunities to maintain and develop their home languages. A **funds of knowledge** approach emphasises the importance of pupils' linguistic and cultural knowledge that is often 'invisible' within our school system. Rather than seeing EAL learners 'in deficit', a funds of knowledge approach focuses on ensuring their home languages and cultures are drawn on as pupils develop PIE through the curriculum. The following case study of one primary school provides examples of this approach to enhancing the learning of a wide range of multilingual learners across the curriculum, as well maintaining and developing communication with the school's parent community.

Case study: our 'language-aware' multilingual learning environment

Information gathering, working with the parent community and establishing a welcoming environment

The school welcomes EAL learners from both settled and newly arrived communities and has a system to gather more information on their multilingual pupil population. The rationale is to both support home learning, as well as positively address the challenge of a high linguistic diversity within and across the school. Some classes have several speakers of the same language, whereas others have a lone native speaker. The School Census data on the number of pupils with EAL and their languages are gathered from parents on admission and supplemented by a school survey on the actual language use of children outside school.

Although undertaken as a whole-school survey in this school, individual teachers can of course build a class 'language profile'. Older pupils may be able to self-report their use of home languages, whereas a letter to parents which explains the purpose of the survey could be used for younger pupils. This communication celebrates and capitalises on families' multilingualism and enhances positive, informal conversations with parents and children. Home language practices and informal learning can include listening to or reading stories in L1, viewing/listening to L1 media and interacting with family or community outside the home (in person or via new technologies). Finding out about any formal learning pupils engage in outside school (e.g. supplementary or community classes) provides further insights into their language and literacy practices.

Activities to promote a 'language-aware' school and class environment

Encouraging children to share information about home language use is a starting point for whole-class discussions and activities; language-awareness raising includes a range of activities focused on learning about the school's multilingual environment:

- making 'Welcome' posters in home languages for school/class display

- gathering data on the number of languages represented

- locating the countries where languages are spoken

- examining the scripts of different languages and comparing these with written English

- listening to excerpts of spoken language and learning language items from pupils such as simple greetings, taking the register in other languages, counting etc.

An initial activity involved pupil investigations into the languages of the school community; a project approach allows children with the language in their repertoire to demonstrate their expertise, as well as to potentially involve other pupils in investigating these and other languages. Sources can include school-based resources, as well of course as opportunities for pupils to draw on the funds of knowledge of parents and the community. Below are examples in poster form of work, some of which include aspects of pupils' identities, as well as factual information (Figure 5.3).

Teachers are sensitive to individual pupil participation and engagement; many pupils are keen to share their home languages, others may be less so. Some pupils may self-report they do not understand or speak another language, which may contradict school records; this may be an effect of transitional

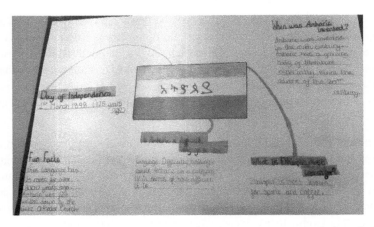

Figure 5.3   Languages project work 'Eritrean' example

bilingualism, whereby some pupils now identify English as their dominant language. Pupils should not feel they need to 'perform' their languages, and 'pupil voice' is the starting point for discussing multilingualism with learners, to set a welcoming and celebratory environment that makes clear all languages are important and valued by the school. Below are some positive aspects, as well as some challenges posed by bilingualism recorded by KS2 children from class discussions (Figures 5.4 and 5.5).

Children and parents are positioned as the 'experts' in a funds of knowledge approach; this has the advantage of enabling teachers to plan activities even when teachers themselves may not have pupils' languages in their own repertoires, which models lifelong learning. Teachers also ensure monolingual English speakers are included, for example an online world languages map 'pinned' with locations and comments; while some pupils highlighted their family journey to the United Kingdom or links with other countries, other children posted about countries they had visited or would like to visit in the future, and the language(s) of those places.

Enhancing home-school links and translanguaging work

The school's support for maintaining children's L1 literacy includes a multilingual 'book club' with dual-language texts. Information gathered on home language use helps guide the purchase of dual language e-books and children and parents are invited to feedback reflections on books enjoyed at home. Over 80 families have used the resource and hard-copy bilingual books can be used in class or borrowed to enjoy at home (Figure 5.6).

Making the most of children's funds of knowledge is evidence from a discussion about forms of politeness in different countries and different conventions around food and sharing meals; children drew and labelled contrasting pictures to share their experiences (Figures 5.7 and 5.8).

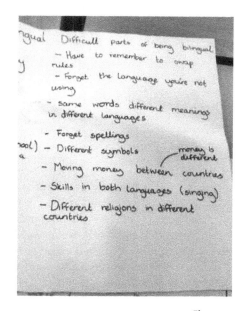
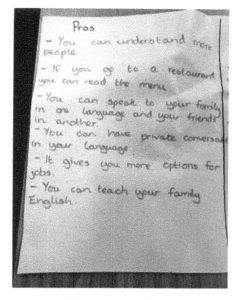

Figures 5.4 and 5.5   Children's perspectives on their bilingualism

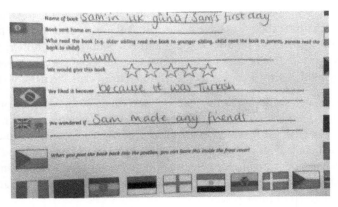

Figure 5.6   Bilingual book club – parent and child feedback on dual language books

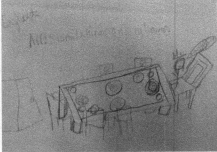

Figures 5.7 and 5.8   Children's drawings of food and sharing meals

Interestingly, the pupil in this example wrote the Arabic label in the Latin alphabet, demonstrating multilingual pupils operate across their languages and literacies in communicative tasks, which is to be welcomed and encouraged.

With thanks to: Abi Blaylock, EAL Coordinator and the staff, pupils and parents of Riverside Primary School, Southwark.

'Language-aware' curricular links

Activities can be planned to enhance cross-curricular work or as a separate project or unit of work; for example, the activities described above include NC links to: Geography skills and knowledge (location, using maps, atlas and globes; human geography features) and Maths (gathering and interpreting data). Religious Education provides natural links for work around multilingualism (e.g. language use in religious contexts) and a PSHE focus on personal development and community cohesion can be enhanced by pupils exploring their language repertoires and that of others. English lessons continuously compare English with pupils' other languages, both in terms of script, grammar and vocabulary features (e.g. etymology of words with shared roots), as well as differences and similarities between language idioms, for example by comparing different well-known sayings.

The other curricular area which can be enhanced by a 'funds of knowledge' approach is Languages (formerly Modern Foreign Language). The current KS2 guidance states:

> *Teaching may be of any modern or ancient foreign language and should focus on enabling pupils to make substantial progress in one language... Language teaching should provide the foundation for learning further languages...*

(DfE, 2013: 194)

While the 2013 NC widened the choice of languages schools may select to teach, its emphasis on 'one language' could lead to a lack of clarity about the position of other languages in the foreign language class, if opportunities for 'translanguaging' are not made and pupils' home languages not also recognised and valued. Costley and Leung highlight a lack of national policy on the use of other languages, which may contribute to teachers' uncertainty on how to approach classroom practice, leaving the impression multilingualism is somehow 'foreign', 'exotic' or related to 'elite' education, as: '...something which happens somewhere else, it is for holidays, it is for future prospects rather than an everyday reality and way of being and doing in the world' (2020: 8). The monolingualism of the NC leads these authors to highlight three key issues:

- as official school language, English is the de facto language of the curriculum, leaving multilingual pupils' knowledges and skills in their languages unrecognised as potentially useful to their learning

- curricular assessment arrangements make no mention of languages other than English and the target MFL

- teachers' perceptions of 'losing control' of the class if they cannot understand pupils' languages

(2020: 10)

These issues mean that schools and teachers in England may not feel prepared to take full advantage of their pupils' multilingualism without enhanced training and curriculum provision.

CHAPTER SUMMARY

Lucas and Villegas' audit (2011: 57) of 'Qualities of Linguistically Responsive Teachers' identifies three key principles for teacher preparation in this new landscape:

- sociolinguistic consciousness (understanding connections between culture, language and identity)
- value for linguistic diversity
- an inclination to advocate for English-language learners

This chapter has sought to support these principles and recognises this area includes complex challenges for Primary teachers. However, the possibilities afforded by a renewed 'broad and balanced curriculum' linked with the increasing diversity of the teaching workforce and schools themselves offer potentially exciting possibilities. By meaningfully celebrating multilingualism in the curriculum through a 'language-aware' pedagogy, we can look forward to enhanced learning in our superdiverse school communities going forward.

Further reading

The Bell Foundation aims to improve school policy, practice and systems for children with English as an additional language. **https://www.bell-foundation.org.uk/eal-programme/**; **https://www.bell-foundation.org.uk**.

Global Story books is a free, research-informed multilingual open-source resource that promotes literacy and language learning in homes, schools and communities. **https://globalstorybooks.net**.

The National Association for Language Development in the Curriculum is the national subject association for EAL. **https://naldic.org.uk**.

References

Anderson, A., Foley, Y., Sangster, P., Edwards, V. and Rassool, N. (2016) *Policy, Pedagogy and Pupil Perceptions: EAL in Scotland and England.* Available at: **https://www.bell-foundation.org.uk/eal-programme/research/policy-pedagogy-and-pupil-perceptions/** (accessed 27 June 2021).

Bell Foundation (2019) *EAL Assessment Framework.* Available at: **https://www.bell-foundation.org.uk/eal-programme/eal-assessment-framework/** (accessed 27 June 2021).

Bell Foundation (2020) *Designing New ITE Curricula: EAL Content Recommendations.* Available at: **https://mk0bellfoundatiw1chu.kinstacdn.com/app/uploads/2020/09/The-Bell-Foundation-ITE-Curricula-Matrix.pdf** (accessed 27 June 2021).

Bradbury, A. (2020) A critical race theory framework for education policy analysis: the case of bilingual learners and assessment policy in England. *Race Ethnicity and Education, 23*(2): 241–260.

Conteh, J. (2019) *The EAL Teaching Book – Promoting Success for Multilingual Learners*, 3rd edition. SAGE/LM. London.

Costley, T. and Leung, C. (2020) Putting ranslanguaging into practice: a view from England. *System, 92*: 102270. **https://doi.org/10.1016/j.system.2020.102270**

Cummins, J. (2017) Teaching minoritized students: are additive approaches legitimate? *Harvard Educational Review, 87*(3): 404–425.

Cummins, J. (2018) Urban multilingualism and educational achievement: identifying and implementing evidence-based strategies for school improvement. In P. Van Avermaet, et al. (eds), *The Multilingual Edge of Education.* London: Palgrave.

DfE (2013) *The National Curriculum in England – Key Stages 1 and 2 Framework Document.* Available at: **https://assets.publishing.service.gov.uk/government/uploads/system/uploads/attachment_data/file/425601/PRIMARY_national_curriculum.pdf** (accessed 11 November 2021).

DfE (2017) *Statutory Framework for the Early Years and Foundation Stage: Setting the Expectations for learning and development for the children from birth to five.* Available at: **https://www.foundationyears.org.uk/files/2017/03/EYFS_STATUTORY_FRAMEWORK_2017.pdf**

DfE (2018) *Newly-Qualified Teachers: Annual Survey 2017 – Research Report.* DFE-RR834. Available at: **https://assets.publishing.service.gov.uk/government/uploads/system/uploads/attachment_data/file/738037/NQT_2017_survey.pdf** (accessed 29 June 2021).

DfE (2019) *Attainment of Pupils With English as an Additional Language- Ad Hoc Notice.* Available at: **https://assets.publishing.service.gov.uk/government/uploads/system/uploads/attach-ment_data/file/908929/Attainment_of_EAL_pupils.pdf** (accessed 4 November 2021).

DfE (2021) *Schools, Pupils and Their Characteristics.* Available at: **https://explore-education-statistics.service.gov.uk/find-statistics/school-pupils-and-their-characteristics** (accessed 20 June 2021).

Foley, Y., Anderson, C., Conteh, J. and Hancock, J. (2018) *Initial Teacher Education and English as an Additional Language.* Available at: **https://www.bell-foundation.org.uk/eal-programme/ research/english-as-an-additional-language-and-initial-teacher-education/** (accessed 27 June 2021)

Gonzalez, N., Moll, L. and Amanti, C. (eds) (2005) *Funds of Knowledge: Theorizing Practices in Households, Communities and Classrooms.* New York, NY: Routledge.

Lucas, T. and Villegas, A. (2011) A framework for preparing linguistically responsive teachers. In T. Lucas (ed.), *Teacher Preparation for Linguistically Diverse Classrooms – A Resource for Teacher Educators.* Abingdon: Routledge.

Strand, S. and Lindorff, A. (2020) *English as an Additional Language: EAL Proficiency in English, Educational Achievement and Rate of Progression in English Language Learning.* Available at: **https://www. bell-foundation.org.uk/eal-programme/research/english-as-an-additional-language-proficiency-in-english-educational-achievement-and-rate-of-progression-in-english-language-learning/** (accessed 27 June 2021)

Vertovec, S. (2007) Super-diversity and its implications. *Ethnic and Racial Studies*, 30(6): 1024–1054.

6

PRESENTING FEMALE PERSPECTIVES

KARIN DOULL

KEYWORDS: FEMININE; GENDER; HISTORICAL CONTEXT; IMBALANCE; PERSPECTIVES; WOMEN'S HISTORY

CHAPTER OBJECTIVES

The aims of this chapter are:

- To place the contributions of women in an historical context.
- To consider how the curriculum can be managed to allow children to recognise and explore female perspectives.
- To suggest some key activities and resources.

CCF ITE links

1.2	Teachers are key role models, who can influence the attitudes, values and behaviours of their pupils.
3.2	Secure subject knowledge helps teachers to motivate pupils and teach effectively.
3.4	Anticipating common misconceptions within particular subjects is also an important aspect of curricular knowledge.
3.7	In all subject areas, pupils learn new ideas by linking those ideas to existing knowledge, organising this knowledge into increasingly complex mental models (or 'schemata'); carefully sequencing teaching to facilitate this process is important.

Introduction

There is no beast, no rush of fire, like woman so untamed. She calmly goes her way where even panthers would be shamed.

Aristophanes, Lysistrata

Women have contributed to and shaped society and yet often this contribution is overlooked or belittled. For much of human history, the primary focus for women was childcare and household management, a necessary provision that allowed men the freedom to explore the world's spectrum. Many of the women that we encounter from previous centuries, therefore, were exceptional, those that were prepared to go their way 'where even panthers would be shamed' (Aristophanes). We know and are uncovering more of the stories of these 'untamed women' but unless we expand our own subject knowledge, we will not be able to introduce them to the children in our schools. We also need to recognise and affirm the experience of the ordinary, the everyday woman. Berkin et al. (2009) identify the need to ensure perspective in order to understand the different contributions made across the full continuum of society. Claire et al. (1993) focus on the need for equality of opportunity to be represented within the curriculum, in relation to content, teaching strategies and individual circumstances.

This chapter considers the role of women across the different curriculum subjects, why and how we should investigate and present their specific perceptions beginning to recognise the 'unacknowledged contribution of women in the past' (Claire, 1996: 8).

Providing a theoretical context

Considering history

'Historians are products of their time and each word is informed by the writer's own experience and background' (Bell et al., 2021). Here Bell et al. identify the essential nature of history in that it is a construct and open to interpretation (Turner-Bissett, 2005). It is not inclusive and immutable but selected and potentially contested. It also reflects the perspectives of the time in which it was constructed (Counsell, 2004; Jordanova, 2006; Lockyer and Tazzyman, 2016; Oslar, 1994). It is key that children understand that our knowledge of the past is created by the narratives we choose to remember. Women's history is not less important or less instructive of the human condition. Until relatively recently history was written by men, and as Lerner (2005) suggests, in defining their own perspectives they have failed to include those of women.

What do we mean by women's history?

When considering a chapter focused on women's history we must confront possibly contentious terms such as feminine/feminism/feminist, gender and women. When we talk about women in this chapter, this encompasses both cis and transgender women. This chapter does not investigate specific histories of transgender women but some consideration on this aspect can be found in Chapter 4. Women's history considers the 'just appreciation, advancement and theoretical understanding of the roles of women' (Corfield, 1999: 339) through the narratives of their lives.

Feminist history has political connotations, dealing as it does with either with early struggles for political and economic equality or a more recent focus on reproductive rights (Jordanova, 2006). It was however the early feminist historians of the 1970s that began to re-discover and re-present stories of women's experiences (Bell et al., 2021; Roper, 2021). These past experiences form the basis of women's history.

The term 'gendered history' should also be considered here. By this we mean the investigation of the relationships between the sexes (Roper, 2021). While the term 'gender' has recently become almost synonymous with biological sex it was previously viewed as a societal construct. It was learned experience based on the expectations, perceived roles and norms of the society of the time (Woolley, 2010). It is important to note that the concept of gender is and always has been fluid and variable (Roper, 2021; Woolley, 2010).

Why have a chapter devoted to women's history?

REFLECTION

What history can you remember doing in school where the focus was primarily on women's experiences?

The question of whether it is valid to have a chapter on women's history was raised by one of the evaluators with the initial proposal for this book. The reviewer suggested that it might be necessary to have a balance, and that the chapter should also consider male stereotypes and injustice because of the need to promote positive role models in the classroom. While we should whole heartedly endorse the need for more men in primary classrooms, this is not the issue in focus here. Winslow (2013) suggests that the inclusion of women's histories or women's studies is about reconciliation not opposition as it represents the experiences of one half of society that has previously not been acknowledged. Claire (1996) highlights the injustice of failing to adequately reflect the experiences of all of humanity suggesting this perpetuates attitudes such as racism and sexism. Bracey et al. concur advocating for 'a more authentic understanding of the past' (2017: 209). Current population data (Ritchie and Roser, 2019) suggest that within Europe and United States females represent just over 50% of the population, effectively the majority. This represents, Lerner suggests, 'half of the world's work and half of the world's experiences' (2005: 169). Unfortunately, these experiences are not always represented within the school curriculum.

The focus of this chapter is the representation of women in history, in terms of inequality and distortion. The observations made here for history could however be replicated across other fields or domains. Bell et al. (2021) suggest that we can find galleries 'full of paintings of women but not by women' (2021: 23), while professors at Yale in 1969 'dismissed even Curie as merely the helper to her husband' when considering the contribution of women scientists (Dominus, 2019). Ashley Fure notes the lack of historic networks and reliance on opaque patronages as previous and continuing issues for female composers (Fure, 2016; Gregory, 2016). Similar constraints restrained the efforts of women across all fields of endeavour. It is often through female agency that these hidden histories become revealed. There is a danger here that a feminist perspective is judged to distort the agenda as there continues to be a prevailing view that 'We associate women [creations] with the female sex and male [creations] with humanity as a whole' (Denjelson in Fure, 2016 no page). This suggests that women's visions or discoveries are of value only to other women (Berkin et al., 2009). Men's experiences have become normative while those of women are reflected through a prism of male values and expectations (Adams, 1983; Bell et al., 2021; Holmes, 2014). Boyd asserts that 'The place of women in the curriculum should need no justification, including the stories and experiences of over half the human race is simply good history' (2019: 16). This validation could be applied to the work of women in all the other domains. If we do not do so, we are in danger of marginalising and devaluing women's cultural contributions (Moorse and Claire, 2007; Tazzyman and Lockyer, 2004).

ACTIVITY

A task that I have often started history sessions with is to ask a group to name a character from history. In a group of 25 you can expect about 3-5 women and probably a similar ration of Black characters. The results will reflect two or three categories:

- *Ruling monarchs* (Elizabeth 1/Victoria/Mary Queen of Scots)
- *Good girls who contribute to society* (Florence Nightingale/Mary Seacole)
- *Those who create a fuss* (Rosa Parks/Emmeline Pankhurst)

(Most Black individuals come from the 20th century such as Martin Luther King)

So, how *do* women get into history?

What does this tell us about the place of women in history?

Can you name women in history not just from 20th/21st centuries?

Can you name any female artists or composers?

Can you link women scientists to your science themes or focus on the work of women mathematicians?

Where is the 'feminine' in the great world religions?

This all becomes even more complex if you try to consider women of colour, lesbian or trans women in these categories.

What evidence do we have for the presence or lack of women in history?

Children experience history through a multitude of sources, films, videos, books, images and artefacts. Where Claire, in the 1990s, suggested how powerful television was in developing children's understanding of history (1996); the focus must now be on social media. Historical gaming is increasingly popular. While such games can provide teachers with some vivid (and generally carefully researched) images of past civilisations (see Assassin's Creed **https://www.ign.com/articles/2018/08/15/ assassins-creed-odyssey-athens** accessed 17 February 2022), they fail to present appropriate protagonists. The lead characters are all focused on power plays and as such 'leave out of the picture the majority of members of past societies' (Biaggi, 2020).

It also has to be said that representations of women in games can be degrading or linked to violence. It is important for teachers to be aware of what sort of history children experience outside school.

Textbooks and websites are used by school to illustrate historical episodes and present factual information. As such they can be seen as authoritative voices of the past, validating certain narratives. It is important to remember that these may have been commissioned to present specific versions, perhaps cultural, ideological or political (Chiponda and Wasserman, 2011). Just as history is a construct, so too are textbooks and web pages, representing as they do a version of the past. Children are not always aware of this accepting the accounts as indisputable, after all 'It was in the textbook' or 'I saw it online'!

Oslar (1994) and Chiponda and Wasserman (2011, 2015) have audited the place of women in history textbooks. This analysis has demonstrated not only an imbalance of female and male presence in history but, more worryingly, subtle degradation in the representation of women. Both language and image are used to suggest the subordinate role of women. In addition, our understanding of the period, person or event can be influenced by the information we take from a visual image (Oslar, 1994). Below are some assumptions that can be created by these practices:

1. Women's history is shown as separate from the mainstream through specific pages related to 'Women in Anglo Saxon England' or 'Woman and work in WW2'. This suggests that women have no place within the dominant male political narrative (Lockyear and Tazzyman, 2016).

2. Women's invisibility is demonstrated on the number of images found within typical classroom textbooks. Oslar (1994), Chiponda and Wasserman (2015) both demonstrated that proportionally speaking fewer women were shown in the pictures in textbooks than men. Of these even fewer women were shown by themselves or as the central character. In the best texts, the ratio is around 2:1 (male:female) while the worst was around 26:1 (Oslar, 1994). This was still true ten years later in Chiponda and Wasserman's studies (2011).

3. Women are presented as having little impact outside the domestic sphere. Images show women within or around the home and engaged in childcare. When shown in conjunction with men they are in a supportive role. They are shown as generally passive and compliant where men are initiators and leaders. Lerner suggests that boys are shown moving from the family into the world but for girls 'family was to be the world' (2005: 162). The *Anglo Saxon Chronicles* tell us that Aethelflaed built forts and conquered cities. A recent primary textbook provided an image of a statue of her with a child. The sword in her other hand seems almost incidental.

4. The language of the supporting text also maintains the narrative of the dominant male (Bell et al., 2021). In suggesting that in Anglo Saxon life men *do the ploughing and planting* while women *look after the children and make clothes*, we present a partial view. It is too simplistic to suggest that women were not also involved in agriculture. In telling the children that women *looked after the house* when men were away, we demean their role. Women would be managing properties including animal and crop husbandry and protecting the home through force of arms if necessary. As teachers we need to be more aware that 'Language, both written and oral is a powerful tool that can be used subjectively, with the ability to locate subjects in positions of power or to demean them' (Chiponda and Wasserman, 2011: 20).

ACTIVITY

Take a textbook from one of your classroom shelves. Count the number of images, drawn or photographs, of people within the book. How many are men only, how many are women with men and how many women by themselves? What is the ratio of images of men to women? In one example recently there were 26 images of men alone, 12 images of men and women and one image of a single women (26:1). Now look at what the images show. What are men doing? What are women doing? How many images are there of women in the dominant position. What does this tell us? What impression does it give us? What subliminal messages is it giving?

What are the implications for including or failing to include women's history?

It is important that children recognise that history is constructed rather than organic and that it is interpretive and changeable rather than fixed. Many children fail to question this but absorb and repeat the narratives provided (Bell et al., 2021). Research among older children has demonstrated the perception that looking at history that has a primarily female focus has less rigour and validity (Berkin et al., 2009). This reinforces the idea, as one student suggested, that 'it was only men that really made an impact' (Holmes, 2014). Levstik's research took this further identifying 'reverse sexism' whereby focusing on women's history excludes the male experience:

> Limiting history to experiences of one gender rather than both meant, they [the students] argued, that they could miss something important.

(Levsik, 2009: 131)

This comment was not raised in relation to history that does not include women, however. This suggests that students see history that involves men as intrinsically more important than that of women. We must begin to encourage children to question this assumption.

Where might we find women in the curriculum?

When planning our history studies, we need to think about how we might integrate women within the curriculum and be aware of the need to make conscious choices linked to a sound historical basis (Pearson, 2012).

Many teachers do not have the time or expertise to create specialised schemes of work. It is therefore important to consider how changes can be made and what additional support and resources will be needed. It may be that the development of women's history within specific primary schools develops at different rates. There are a number of different levels of engagement (Turnica, 1992). These are not progressive or mutually exclusive. The focus may shift for different teachers or with different units of study.

Much women's history relates to the exceptional, those women who meet conventional criteria for recognition. It is important to realise that the experiences of these women exclude the realities for the bulk of the female population (Lerner, 2005; Tudor, 2002). We should remember 'It is not just great events that shape the world, but the seemingly insignificant daily routine in which we all take part' (Mather, 2014: no page). There is a place for social and cultural history that allows us to explore these dimensions.

Mainstream women's history within primary schools generally focuses on the fight for women's suffrage, women's 'work' and standout individuals. We can look separately at the unique experiences of women but this might be divisive suggesting that their past is not part of the norm (Oslar, 1994; Tudor, 2002). We might also seek to add women's narratives to mainstream but here their experiences might be subsumed into or lost in the wider whole (Boyd, 2019; Tudor, 2002).

Table 6.1 delineates the different levels in which women's history can be integrated into the curriculum.

Table 6.1 Some patterns of delivery for women's history

Definition (Boyd, 2019)	Definition (Tunica in Oslar, 1994)		Examples
Conforming	Distinct	Those who by virtue of birth or wealth are able to affect circumstances around them and create a name within history, the exceptional, the firsts.	Hashepsut (Ancient Egypt) Florence Nightingale
Contributory	Reforming	Those who worked alongside men, (supported perhaps by fathers or brothers) and achieved acclaim through their activities in conjunction with them. They might be considered within the perspective of the dominant group.	Caroline Herschel, Clara Schumann Boudicca from the point of view of the Romans
Compensatory	Affirming	Investigating histories that consider women's experiences in their own right	Project on 'Women in space' (KS2) or 'Washday' (KS1)
Challenge	Challenge	Stories that challenge the existing order setting questions for the children to identify who is missing from history and why this is so. Problem-solving research challenges	Consider the fight against the Great Viking Army from the point of view of Aethelflaed (KS2) Investigate a female local campaigner – Charlotte Despard (KS1)
Integrated	Transforming	Balanced curriculum reconceptualised with inclusive core	Project on the fight for human rights from Magna Carter through Chartism/Tolpuddle Martyrs/ Abolition/Trade Unionism/Women's Suffrage with focus on women's involvement throughout.

──── **REFLECTION** ────

Look at which individuals are named in your curriculum plans. In identifying key individuals to be studied, what proportion of these are women? Can you expand this to include more women?

How might we begin to redress the balance?

It is important to consider what is already in place within the school alongside your own subject knowledge. Here are a few action you could take.

1. Consider your own subject knowledge and plan how you might develop this.

2. Undertake an audit of curriculum coverage through policy documents, curriculum maps and schemes of work. What is already there and what needs development?

3. Next look at the resources that are available (in school already) and those that are most used. What images, documents and artefacts do you use that reflect women's history. What do you need?

4. Audit the knowledge of the staff. Where do they bring in women's history? Who do they focus on? Why do they mention these individuals? Is there a reason why they do not have a female perspective within their history projects?

5. Consider the type of women's history you want to promote within the school (see above). How far do you want to go here?

6. Research some resources that will support this and present ideas for discussion with staff.

──── **REFLECTION** ────

Consider the school's curriculum map

•   Why have certain foci been chosen? Why, for example, have you chosen this aspect on Ancient Egypt?
•   What element of change within living memory have you selected?
•   Do the substantive concepts allow us also to consider women's experiences? How do 'trade', 'invasion', 'settlement' or 'power' allow for female perspectives?

What does Ofsted advocate?

The Ofsted Research Review for History is clear about the role of class teachers and subject leaders in curriculum design. It is not so much what is included within the curriculum that is important but being able to justify the choices we make about what to include.

They do highlight the need to ensure that there is a breadth as well as depth in the curriculum, that 'the diversity of the past is represented in the curriculum content' (Ofsted, 2021: 29). It is also important to consider a curriculum that relates to 'pupils' identity and experience' while connecting this to 'overview knowledge of the past' (Ofsted, 2021: 30).

A social history perspective within one of the period studies for Key Stage 2 will allow children to develop wide 'hinterland' knowledge (as advocated by Ofsted) while also allowing children to reflect on women's experiences.

FINDING RESOURCES

Here are some useful websites as starting points:

https://www.bbc.co.uk/teach/teach/womens-history-month-international-womens-day/z7rr6v4

Links to BBC resources which are specifically primary school-based

https://womenshistorynetwork.org/links-to-useful-resources-and-information-that-will-help-teachers-to-promote-womens-history-in-the-classroom/

Many of these resources will be adult or secondary level. They provide images and documents that you can adapt and use with primary children. They also provide background subject knowledge for you

https://cdn.nationalarchives.gov.uk/documents/education/womens-history-resource.pdf

This is an aid that directs you to the resources created by The National Archives related to women's history.

When you buy books for your class or library, look for picture books that tell women's stories. For example, Kate Pankhurst's series 'Great Women who...' are ideal for the reading corner. For older children you could look at Roy Charles's *Great British Women* (2021).

Some final thoughts

Three key ideas to think about in relation to women's history.

- 'The rise of women's and gender history has coincided with the arrival of women in positions of economic and political power' (Roper, 2021: no page)

- 'Absence of evidence is not evidence of absence' (Bell et al., 2021: 93)

- 'When women aren't there why is that?' (Tudor, 2002: 30)

I have always been interested in stories about the other experiences of women. My undergraduate dissertation was an oral history investigation on 'The Fisherwomen of North East Scotland'. Those who read primary history will see that my articles almost always have a feminine element if not focus. I think I have to agree with Jordanova in saying 'I am a feminist historian because thinking about gender relations ... from a women's point of view has been a central part of my life' (2006: 2).

Having considered the theory how could we put these ideas into practice? Here are some examples of possible activities.

Case studies

Recreating the dinner party: a whole school project

In 1979, Judy Chicago created an art installation that celebrated women's history. Each woman at the table was presented through a plate and a textile place setting. I took part in a project to recreate this. My chosen lady was Bessie Coleman, the first Black woman to gain her pilot's licence, a passionate advocate of education, racial equality and flying. Several schools also took part asking children to consider who they would choose and why they felt these should be included (Figure 6.1).

I have used this idea with students asking them to select a character, include an image of her, some general information and a quote about or by her. We made use of pillow cases to provide a common background. Images could be sewn, pasted or stencilled on (Figure 6.2).

This would make a fascinating whole school project for Women's History Day (or Month) asking each class to select a woman. I would encourage staff to try to seek out those local to the school or linked to different spheres of endeavour. I would also try to avoid the less well-known. I think Florence Nightingale has had enough publicity unless we feature her as a mathematician.

Historical learning: Here you are focusing on the disciplinary concepts of *significance* and *historical interpretation* while *selecting and combining information*.

You could present in a timeline so reinforcing *chronological understanding*.

Figure 6.1   Plate and runner representing Bessie Coleman

Figure 6.2   Images of student's work

Washday (EYs and KS1)

Source a number of artefacts or contact your local museum to see if they have a handling collection.

Use images and talk about how we wash and iron clothes today. Take children through the process. Who does the washing in your house? What do you use to do the washing? What do you need to do the washing? How long does it take? If you have a washing machine on school site, take the children and put a load on.

Now present the children with artefacts:

Bar of soap and grater, wash board, tongs, clothes wringer, iron, metal or enamel wash tub if possible (Figure 6.3).

We are going to do some washing. How shall we do that? Get the children to investigate the artefacts and then get them to suggest how they might be used. You will need to do some problem-solving. How do I get the water into the tub? How do I make the water soapy? What will happen if I try to get the clothes out of the hot water? How will I get the water out of the clothes? (Do be careful of any wringers and only let adults use this as children often get their fingers trapped.) How long do you think this took?

Figure 6.3   A display of household artefacts from the 1950s

You can use the picture book *Peepo!* (Janet and Allan Ahlberg)

Try to get someone to come in and talk about what it was like washing without a washing machine.

Historical learning: Here you are looking at the disciplinary concepts of *change and continuity* and *characteristic features* while asking children to make some *deductions from the resources*. You are also making use of *subject-specific vocabulary*.

Exploring the explorers using picture books (KS1)

Source picture books about female explorers or travellers. Children work in pairs or groups to find out about their character. They need to create a 3D artefact to show what they have learnt. They must explain why this person wanted to explore and why they should be remembered (Figure 6.4).

Historical learning: Here you are looking at the disciplinary concepts of *cause and consequence* and *significance* while *selecting and combining information*.

Making connections across the ancient civilisations: ruler, priestess, warrior (KS2)

Split the class into three groups and each group takes a separate civilisation and specific individual. (You could also look at Indus Valley civilisation but we know less about these and there are no named individuals.)

1.   Hatshepsut – Ancient Egypt

2.   Enheduanna – Ancient Sumar

3.   Lady Fu Hao – Shang Dynasty

Figure 6.4   These photos show student's representation of the explorers Mae Jamison, Alexandra David Neel,
Harriet Charmers Adams and Mary Kingsley

Ask children to research key aspects of these women and their civilisations. What was their role/s. How do we know about them? What memorials did they leave behind? Create a web page for a class website. Create a class page to draw together observations comparing the three women and civilisations.

What is significant about these women? What do they tell us about the roles that women could play in their civilisations? What similarities and differences do we find? We can find women in ancient Egypt playing a similar role to Enheduanna (Meresamun). Pu'abi in Ancient Sumar had a similar tomb burial to that of Lady Fu Hao. There are suggestions that Hatshepsut may have led the army into battle although she was never really a warrior queen.

CHAPTER SUMMARY

Children are inclined to think that the lack of women in history is because they were less important or worthwhile. This is reinforced by either the invisibility of women completely or the type of representations within textbooks and online resources. In ignoring women's history, we negate the lives and experience so over 50% of humankind. We narrow the possibilities for investigation and exploration. In seeking to redress the balance we need to think carefully about how we might want to do this. This could be through a focus on exceptional women; through adding women into the existing narrative, either considering their experiences in isolation or in seeking to insert them into male perspectives; by teaching gendered history that explores the relationships between men and women's histories. Until relatively recently women were present but anonymous in history. Their stories are out there but often need to be found; evidence needs to be stitched together. It is important to redress the balance.

Further reading

Andrews, M. and Lomas, J. (2018) *A History of Women in 100 Objects*. Stroud: The History Press.

Bell, J., Hershaman, T. and Holland, A. (2021) *On This Day She: Putting Women Back in History One Day at a Time*. London: Metro Publishing.

Charles, R. (2021) *Great British Women*. Edinburgh: White on Black Publishing.

References

Adams, C. (1983) Off the record. *Teaching History, 36*: 3–6.

Ahlberg, A. and Janet (2011) *Peepo*. London: Penguin Books.

Aristophanes (411BC) Lysistrata Lines 1014 – 1017. Available at: **http://johnstoniatexts.x10host.com/aristophanes/lysistratahtml.html** (accessed January 2022).

Bell, J., Hershman, T. and Holland A. (2021) *On This Day She ... Putting Women Back Into History One Day at a Time*. London: Metro Publishing.

Berkin, C., Crocco, M. and Windslow, B. (2009) *Clio in the Classroom: A Guide for Teaching US Women's History*. New York, NY: Oxford University Press.

Biaggi, C. (2020) *Can Video Games Improve History Education?* Available at: **https://www.euroclio.eu/2020/03/24/can-video-games-improve-history-education/** (accessed December 2021).

Boyd, S. (2019) From "great women" to an inclusive curriculum: how should women's history be included at KS3? *Teaching History, 175*: 17–19.

Bracey, P., Jackson, D. and Gove-Humphries, A. (2017) Diversity in history education. In I. Davies (ed.), *Debates in History Teaching*, 2nd edition. Abingdon: Routledge, pp. 202–212.

Charles, R. (2021) *Great British Women*. Edinburgh: White on Black Publishing.

Chiponda, A. and Wasserman, J. (2011) Women in history textbooks: what messages does this send to the youth? *Yesterday and Today*, 6(1): 3–25.

Chiponda, A. and Wasserman, J. (2015) An analysis of the visual portrayal of women in junior secondary Malawian school history textbooks. *Yesterday and Today*, 14: 208–237.

Claire, H. (1996) *Reclaiming Our Pasts – Equality and Diversity in the Primary Curriculum*. Stoke on Trent: Threntham Books Ltd.

Claire, H., Maybin J. and Swann, J. (1993) *Equality Matters: Case Studies From the Primary School*. Clevedon: Multilingual Matters.

Corfield, P. (1999) From women's history to gender history: a reply to playing the gender history game. *Rethinking History*, 3(3): 339–341.

Counsell, C. (2004) Looking through a Josephine Butler shaped window: focussing pupils' thinking on historical significance. *Teaching History*, 114: 30–34.

Dominus, S. (2019) Women scientists were written out of history. It's Margaret Rossiter's mission to fix that. *Smithsonian Magazine*. Available at: **https://www.smithsonianmag.com/science-nature/unheralded-women-scientists-finally-getting-their-due-180973082/** (accessed December 2021).

Fure, A. (2016) *Reflections on Risk*. Available at: **https://griddarmstadt.wordpress.com/2016/08/14/reflections-on-risk-by-ashley-fure/** (accessed December 2021).

Gregory, A. (2016) A history of classical music (the women-only version) *NY Times December*. Available at: **https://www.nytimes.com/interactive/2016/12/02/arts/music/01womencomposers.html** (accessed December 2021).

Holmes, K. (2014, April 14) *Moving Beyond Boundaries – Student Perspective*. Available at: **https://teachingwomenshistory.com/moving-beyond-boundaries-project-blog/**

Jordanova, L. (2006) *History in Practice*, 2nd edition. London: Bloomsbury.

Lerner, G. (2005) *The Majority Finds Its Past*. London: University of North Carolina.

Levstik, L. (2009) Well behaved women rarely make history: gendered teaching and learning in and about history. *International Journal of History*, 8(1): 120–139.

Lockyear, B. and Tazzyman A. (2016) Victims of history: challenging students perspectives of history. *Teaching History*, 165: 8–15.

Mather, R. (2014, March 20) *What Moving Beyond the Boundaries Means for Me*. Available at: **https://teachingwomenshistory.com/moving-beyond-boundaries-project-blog/**

Moorse, K. and Claire, H. (2007) History in Myers, K., et al. (2007) *Genderwatch, Still Watching*. Stoke on Trent: Trentham.

Ofsted (2021) *Ofsted Research Review for History*. Available at: **https://www.gov.uk/government/publications/research-review-series-history** (accessed December 2021)

Oslar, A. (1994) Still hidden from history? The representation of women in recently published history textbooks. *Oxford Review of Education*, 2(2): 219–235.

Pearson, J. (2012) Where are we? The place of women in history curricular. *Teaching History, 147*: 47–52.

Ritchie, H. and Roser, M. (2019) *Gender Ratio Our World in Data*. Available at: **https://ourworldindindata.org/gender-ratio**

Roper, L. (2021) *The Growth of Gender and Woman's History*. Available at: **https://www.history.ox.ac.uk/growth-gender-and-womens-history** (accessed November 2021)

Tazzymann, A. and Lockyear, B. (2014, March 6) *What Did Women Do ?* Available at: **https://teachingwomenshistory.com/moving-beyond-boundaries-project-blog/**

Tudor, R. (2002) Teaching the history of women in Europe in the twentieth century. *Teaching History, 107*: 22–33.

Turner-Bisset, R. (2005) *Creative Teaching : History in the Primary School*. London: David Fulton.

Turnica, N. (1992) Joan makes history: looking at gender issues in the teaching of history. *Teaching History Journal of History Teachers Association of NSW, 26*(3): 34–37.

Winslow, B. (2013) Clio in the curriculum: the state of women and women's history in the middle and high school curriculum… and perhaps a way forward. *Journal of Women's History, 25*(4): 319–332.

Woolley, R. (2010) *Tackling Controversial Issues in the Primary School*. London: Routledge.

7

THE SIGNIFICANCE OF PEOPLE IN THE PAST

BENTE OPHEIM

KEYWORDS: CAUSE; CHANGE; CONSEQUENCE; CONTINUITY; DIVERSITY; ETHICS; EVIDENCE; INCLUSION; PERSPECTIVE; SIGNIFICANCE

CHAPTER OBJECTIVES

The aims of this chapter are:

- To recognise that historical significance is constructed and given meaning in a particular narrative.
- To consider the ethical dimension of reconstructing the past.
- To provide an example of how to work with census material and historical thinking in the classroom.

CCF ITE links

3.2	Secure subject knowledge helps teachers to motivate pupils and teach effectively.
3.5	Explicitly teaching pupils the knowledge and skills they need to succeed within particular subject areas is beneficial.
3.6	In order for pupils to think critically, they must have a secure understanding of the knowledge within the subject area they are being asked to think critically about.
3.7	In all subject areas pupils learn new ideas by linking to existing knowledge, organising this knowledge into increasingly complex mental models or schemata.

Introduction

'Histories are the stories we tell about the past': This is Peter Seixas and Tom Morton's point of departure as they explain what historical thinking is (Seixas and Morton, 2013). Yet, those stories are also about the present. Everything we are and do in the present is the result of the past, and our only way to make meaningful connections between the past and the present is through the stories we tell about the past. When doing history – i.e. telling stories about the past – we make choices based on content knowledge and interpretation of evidence. When we teach history, we tend to present stories about the past without revealing all the choices and considerations we have made in the process, but the choices in themselves are a gateway to historical thinking. Teaching history, as pointed out by a number of scholars, should also involve activities which not only enhances content knowledge but also engender historical thinking, understood through concepts such as historical significance, evidence, continuity and change, cause and consequence, perspectives and ethics (Seixas and Morton, 2013).

This chapter will demonstrate how census data about a particular 19th century townhouse can be used to create different stories about the house and its inhabitants. The chapter exemplifies how the process of creating historical narratives in the classroom helps the children to understand that historians make choices in terms of what we include in our stories as well as how we tell them. Awareness of such choice-making is imperative to the awareness of inclusion and diversity, as it raises the questions of whose history we choose to tell and why it is important to tell it.

Why use census data when teaching history?

Historical knowledge is contingent on a critical use of evidence, and the importance of using primary sources has been a recurring theme for reformers of history curricula for the last century (Sandwell and Heyking, 2014). Professionals have, nevertheless, disagreed on whether students can learn and master the skills needed to make sound judgements of historical evidence. Some even argue that only very few students are able to grasp the complexity of the kind of source criticism involved in making claims about the past (Lévesque, 2008). Yet others have claimed that children as young as seven years old can understand that selection and interpretation of evidence can lead to different histories being told. The most recent body of research, mainly from the United States and Canada, seem to support the assertion that children and adolescences may engage in historical investigations in effective and meaningful ways when given appropriate time and opportunity (Lévesque, 2008). Nevertheless, many children spend a lot of time learning about history without ever being introduced to primary sources. According to Sears, they have not 'had to think historically, but rather have been relatively passive observers to others' attempts to do so' (Sears, 2014: 130). Addressing this, Gibson (2014) has argued that teachers and student teachers need to reflect on, and actively engage in, designing classroom activities that effectively use historical evidence. She found, from her own research, that student teachers encountered a number of obstacles when designing activities using historical sources, and that the preparation of pre-service teachers must not assume that the student teachers' prior experience or education will provide them with enough understanding of the discipline of history (Gibson, 2014). It requires disciplinary content knowledge and skills that may be perceived as counterintuitive or 'unnatural', as Wineburg has put it.

Census data are about people in the past; people with names, addresses and very often occupations or family positions. The census data used in the examples recount individuals' positions in households, making it possible to trace people life histories through different censuses. This enables us to see how living conditions and circumstances change through time, as households grow, move or split up, and individuals get married, have children or die. Such data can often be supplemented by parish records which can hold information about christenings, weddings, burials and other events where the church officials have been involved. Thus, census data give us a glimpse into real lives of in the past, linked to real places in local communities, all of which can heighten our sense of connection to history.

Connecting to something local and tangible has often been emphasised when working with young children. It helps them understand the relevance of history when people of the past have names, places and life stories connected to them. Even older pupils have reported that personal stories interest them the most, and we may all have experienced teachers and textbooks recounting the life and deeds of great men of the past. However, census data offer a way to bring the unknown stories of the ordinary, the less wealthy, the marginalised into the classroom, thus inviting a whole range of questions concerning gender, age, ethnicity or abilities of people in the past.

REFLECTION

Census and parish records are documentary sources of primary evidence that generally need to be sourced by the teacher. Think about whether you remember using such evidence yourself. What do you think might be an issue, either for the teacher or pupil's with its use?

Why use life histories?

According to Bage (1999), 'History is the construction and deconstruction of explanatory narratives about the past, derived from evidence and in answer to questions. This can be explained to children as finding answers to questions and questions to answer, by taking apart and putting together again real stories about the past'. Life stories built on evidence from primary sources can offer the kind of real stories that will engage children's interest in the past and encourage them to raise new questions.

In the following section, you will find the stories of one household. In considering the different perspectives we present different versions of the past. This selection can present a distorted view of that past that fails to present the life stories of different elements of society. This can suggest that those stories are of little or lesser value, thereby presenting history where male-centred is normative.

The story about a prosperous merchant

There is already a story connected to the Villa, told by local historians and available to teachers and students by a few mouse clicks. The builder and first owner of the Villa was Harald Irgens, a well-known owner of a shipping company in Bergen. He came from a prominent local family of politicians and entrepreneurs and worked his way up the social ladder. A search through the Digital Archive of census and parish records gives a fairly comprehensive outline of his biography. He married his cousin Marie, and they became parents to their first child in 1863. Two years later, the family is registered as tenants to a baker. His household also includes two servants, and he is registered as clerk at a shipping company. Ten years later, in the 1875 census, his household has grown as five more children have been born, and the number of servants doubled. His title is now 'merchant and ship owner', and the family has moved into their own townhouse. Another 10 years on, nine children are registered to that address. At this time, at the end of the 1880s, the plans to build Villa Fredheim materialised and Harald, nearing the age of 70, move into the Villa with his wife and five of his children.

The personal story of Harald Irgens success, which can be pieced together from the sources, is connected to a larger story of Bergen as a port of trade and shipping in the second half of the 19th century. The city experienced a boom in shipping industry as sail ships were replaced by steamers. This also opened up for involvement in new foreign trade markets such as the fruit import from South America. Harald Irgens' shipping company was heavily involved in fruit export from Cuba to the United States. Thus, the story of Harald Irgens and his shipping company is closely connected to a period in the city's history dominated by expansion and economic growth. As such, it is also an example of a general characteristic of Norway in the second half of 19th century, a period of industrialisation and rapid rise in population. In this way, the individual story can serve as an example of regional and national historical development. It is, nevertheless, as story told from the perspective of an upper-class, male protagonist. What could the world look like from the perspective of his wife?

The merchant's child-rearing wife

The census and parish records show that Christine Marie was only twenty years old when she married Harald. She, being his cousin, had the same social background as her husband. But whereas he was busy building up an international shipping company, she was busy child-rearing. Christine and Harald had 13 children over a span of 22 years. This meant that she was constantly pregnant or had an infant to look after, or both, during those years. The first child, Ole, died when he was eight months old, and by that time Christine was already six months pregnant with the second child. Four of their children died young, leaving the couple with 9 living children when the last one was born. At that point Christine was 43 years old.

Christine's story is by no means exceptional. Infant mortality was high at this time, but a common misconception is that this was first and foremost linked to poverty. Women from the upper classes were married young because their families could afford it. Therefore, they also gave birth to many children, and although they could provide better conditions for their children, they could not shield their family members from contagious diseases or infections. The parish sources that recount the deaths for each year seldom report cause of death, but one will notice that the numbers are unpredictable, with high peaks at irregular intervals. This indicates that a significant number of the deaths are linked to the spread of contagious diseases, such as the measles, which was dreaded by any parent.

Christine's story gives us a glimpse into a woman's upper-class life in the second half of the 19th century. Her life story is by no means remarkable but can inform of us about demography and living conditions in the past, and serve as an example of how those conditions had an impact on someone's life.

The child

One of Christine and Harald's children was a girl named Marie. In several of the records she is only referred to as 'Mimmi', and in two of the photos available to the public, she appears to be suffering from some kind of disease affecting her stature. When tracing her records, one will also find that she never married and continued to live in her parents' household her entire life, which ended at a sanitorium for patients diagnosed with tuberculosis at an age of 51. At the first sight, the pieces of information we have about Mimmi seem to support a well-established supposition that people with disabilities were marginalised and lived hard lives. Many certainly did, but compared to her sister, and what we know of the 19th century Norway, there is nothing out of the ordinary in Mimmi's life story. Her name is a very common nickname for variants of the name Marie and also appear as a given name to over 6,000 women in Norway in 1870. The fact that she never married is also not very particular. Her older sister was also unmarried and lived with her parents all her life, as did many women of the urban upper class. The number of unmarried women were rising in the second half of the 19th century, and women without husbands were granted new legal and economic rights, enabling them to provide for themselves. Admittingly, Mimmi did not live a long life, and she died from tuberculosis, but her sister also died at a fairly young age, 47, of unknown cause. The point is that there is nothing in the historical evidence to suggest that Mimmi lived a life full of hardship due to her physical disabilities. We just do not know that. But it raises a lot of interesting questions about values and norms and rights that help us understand the past in terms of diversity and inclusion.

REFLECTION

What do these stories leave you still wanting to know? What questions remain? How might you help children understand about the fragmentary nature of historical evidence?

Working with multiple life stories in the classroom as historical thinking competencies

When pupils are engaged in the process of piecing together the life story of a given individual of the past, they are immediately facing the question of *significance*. How can this, perhaps completely unknown and insignificant person have any historical significance to us? The question of historical significance is very often ignored by students and teachers because the answer seems so obvious: we teach and learn about historical figures because they were significant. But who decided to bestow such significance to people of the past and by whose standards? As Seixas and Morton (2013) have put it: when pupils are taught to think critically about what is historically significant, they learn not only about the past but also more importantly how to make reasoned decisions about historical significance, as an historian would do.

There are several criteria one may use to assign significance to events and people of the past. A well-known method is to establish whether the person or event of the past caused change or had long-lasting effects on society. The story of the merchant who found a new trading niche at a crucial time in process of modernisation of the merchant fleet is such a story of change and had long-lasting effects. However, the story does not have room for his wife nor his children. That does not mean that they are historically insignificant, but we must restore to a different kind of historical significance, one that focuses on people or events that shed light on important changes or processes. The story of the merchants' wife connects to social structures and conditions of life important for the understanding of late 19th century Norway. She was a woman, a wife and a mother, but first and foremost she was an historical agent who faced circumstances and made decisions which had significant consequences. The lesson to learn about this kind of historical significance is that it is assigned by the creator of the historical narrative, or in this case by the children themselves. We make something significant by giving credit to remarkable people of the past or people whose story can tell us something about the past.

While the histories of the merchant and his wife may be deemed significant because their actions changed or shed light on changes in the past, the history of the child is significant because of the lack of such recognition in the past. She was deemed unimportant and insignificant in her own lifetime. Her historical significance is rather brought about as an ethical response to changing attitudes of the present. Thus, this example also serves to underline that historical significance is contextual. It is to some extent determined by what writers and data collectors in the past valued and deemed significant to preserve, but it is also, to a large extent, determined by what historians, teachers and learners deem valuable and significant at the present. Awareness among learners that historical significance is constructed in relation to today's concerns can help them understand how significance varies over time and according to the perspective of different groups (Seixas and Morton, 2013). Such awareness of historical significance is a challenging competence for learners to meet, making it no less important for educators to pay attention to (Lévesque, 2008).

Ideas for classroom activities and potential resources

The outlined life histories described above is a result of pupils working in groups, piecing together information about different people connected to each other as part of the same family or belonging to the same household, or living in the same house. The learnings have to make choices about what to include, which path to explore and what to leave behind, according to what they deem significant. The end result is not one story about a family but several stories that give different perspectives on life in a 19th century household. This method makes room for a diverse and inclusive narrative of the past, that recognise the interpretative and ethical dimension of how history comes about.

The histories may be presented in written form, or orally, or by means of digital tools, and is suitable for projects which integrate learning outcomes from several subjects. Digital storytelling is an effectful way to also work with historical images, and let the pupils narrate the stories using their own voices. It is a good idea to have the pupils write a storyboard for their digital story, where they discuss what to include, how and why. This highlights the awareness of what is significant to include and why. Such a storyboard may also function as a way to assess the pupils and to give formative response to their work.

REFLECTION

Why should we seek out a range of stories that present different perspectives? How do we help children make judgements about significance? What criteria do we use to judge significance?

CHAPTER SUMMARY

This chapter has used the parallel stories of one merchant family in Bergen, Norway to illustrate how selection and significance can shape the history that we experience. In choosing which story to focus on we illuminate a different aspect of life at that time. It is these choices, made by historians, that create an historical narrative. Significance, as Counsell (2004) and Lomas (2019) suggest, should not be uncontested, allowing us to select evidence to fill in the outline of history. This chapter has helped demonstrate how a more inclusive history can be presented through focusing on a broader selection of sources.

Further reading

Doull, K., Russell, C. and Hales, A. (2020) *Mastering Primary History*. London: Bloomsbury.

Percival, J. (2021) *Understanding and Teaching Primary History*. London: SAGE.

Temple, S. (2013) Using archives creatively. In H. Cooper (ed.), *Teaching History Creatively*. Abingdon: Routledge, pp. 51–64.

References

Bage, G. (1999) *Narrative Matters: Teaching and Learning History Through Story*. London: Falmer Press.

Counsell, C. (2004) Looking through a Josephine-Butler-shaped window: focusing pupils' thinking on historical significance. *Teaching History, 114*: 30–34.

Gibson, L. (2014) Teaching student teachers to use primary sources when teaching history. In R. Sandwell and A.V. Heyking (eds), *Becoming a History Teacher – Sustaining Practices in Historical Thinking and Knowing*. Toronto, ON: Toronto University Press.

Lévesque, S. (2008) *Thinking Historically: Educating Students for the Twenty-First Century*. Toronto, ON: University of Toronto Press.

Lomas, T (2019) Getting to grips with concepts in primary history. *Primary History Journal, 82*: 9–16.

Sandwell, R. and Heyking, A.V. (2014) *Becoming a History Teacher: Sustaining Practices in Historical Thinking and Knowing*. Toronto, ON: University of Toronto Press.

Sears, A. (2014) Moving form the periphery to the core: the posssiblilities for professional learning communities. In R. Sandwell and A.V. Heyking (eds), *Becoming a History Teacher*. Toronto, Buffalo, London: Toronto University Press.

Seixas, P. and Morton, T. (2013) *The Big Six: Historical Thinking Concepts*. Toronto, ON: Nelson Education.

8

AN IRISH DIMENSION WITHIN THE PRIMARY HISTORY CURRICULUM

PAUL BRACEY

KEYWORDS: DIVERSITY; IRELAND; MIGRATION; MULTICULTURAL BRITAIN; 'THESE ISLANDS'

CHAPTER OBJECTIVES

The aims of this chapter are:

- To provide an understanding of how an Irish dimension relates to diversity.
- To provide a rationale for integrating an Irish dimension into the history curriculum.
- To provide an understanding of ways in which an Irish dimension can be integrated into the primary curriculum.

CCF ITE links

1.5	A culture of mutual trust and respect supports effective relationships.
3.4	Anticipating common misconceptions within particular subjects is also an important aspect of curriculum knowledge.
3.6	In order for pupils to think critically, they must have a secure understanding of the knowledge within the subject area they are being asked to think critically about.
4.7	High quality classroom talk can support pupils to articulate key ideas, consolidate understanding and extend their vocabulary.

Introduction

Why should we consider Ireland when teaching for diversity?

The Black Lives Matter Movement has drawn attention for the need to ensure that a Black dimension should be given an appropriate place in the school history curriculum. This chapter fully supports this but argues that teaching diversity needs to go beyond a Black/white binary perspective. It will demonstrate how an Irish dimension in the history curriculum contributes to a broadly based understanding of the past. The need to appreciate this is evident in issues associated with Britain's departure from the European Union and its implications for people living in Northern Ireland. The Irish community is the largest ethnic minority community in our society. These factors reflect the proximity of Ireland to Britain together with the historical relationship between them. You may at this point wonder how this relates to your role as a primary teacher. The complexities of this sensitive and controversial topic include some issues and contexts which are beyond the remit for primary age children. This also applies to other sensitive and controversial topics such as the Holocaust or slavery. However, it will be argued that, provided the context and approach used are related to the age of the children, such topics are appropriate to their developmental needs.

The following sections will include a consideration of the way in which an Irish dimension has been related to our multicultural society, ways in which it has been related to teaching for diversity and the implications of this for the primary school history curriculum.

An Irish dimension and diversity in the curriculum: issues and opportunities

The following quotations related to different points over the past 50 years provide a useful insight into the above question:

Slater (1989) commenting on the period preceding 1970 argued that:

> Content was largely British, or rather Southern English; Celts looked in to starve, emigrate or rebel... abroad was of interest once it was part of the Empire, foreigners were sensibly allies or rightly defeated.
>
> (Slater, 1989: 1, cited in Phillips, 1998: 14)

The implication from this statement was that the curriculum needed to address the way in which aspects of the past including Ireland were taught. In 2000, the Parekh Report produced a vision of multicultural Britain which challenged traditional perceptions of British identity and history. Within this construct it argued:

> The position of the Irish as insider-outsider is uniquely relevant to the nature of its multicultural society. For generations, Irish experience has been neglected owing to the myth of homogeneity of white Britain, but it also illuminated Britishness in much the same way that the experience of black people illuminates whiteness.
>
> (Parekh, 2000: 32)

The implication is that an Irish dimension's contribution to our diverse society needed to be acknowledged. Seven years later, the Ajegbo et al. Report (2007) included the following reference to an Irish dimension as a means of supporting community cohesion.

Pupils should explore the chronological makeup of the UK by recognising that the UK is made up of four individual nations, each having its own history, heritage, and traditions.

(Ajegbo et al., 2007: 101, Appendix 1)

More recently, the Sewell Report (2021) recommended:

We believe that young people are entitled to a wider understanding of the UK which encompasses the local cultures of regions such as the North or the Midlands, the 4 nations that form the UK, as well as the Commonwealth and former colonies such as the West Indies, India, and Pakistan. These countries and local areas have historically been 'defined' by their connection to the UK, but equally have played their role in defining 'Britishness' today.

(Sewell et al., 2021: 90)

Each of these statements reflects distinctive contexts. Slater was referring to a period associated with the end of the British Empire. The three reports relate to issues not directly linked to Ireland – the Parekh Report followed the Macpherson Report which challenged Institutional Racism in response to the handling of the death of a Black teenager called Stephen Lawrence, and the Ajegbo Report was concerned with community cohesion following the London Tube bombings by terrorists in 2007. The Sewell Report followed Black Lives Matter Protests in 2020. All three reports proved contentious with significant differences in the perspectives held between Sewell and its predecessors. However, all of them called for a broader understanding of our diverse society and included reference to an Irish dimension. Given that the same issue has been repeatedly raised over such a long period of time raises questions about their impact. Consequently, this raises questions about how far this has been reflected in the history curriculum and that of the broader primary curriculum as a whole.

REFLECTION

How does an Irish dimension to issues related to developing an understanding of our multicultural society?

Developing an Irish dimension in school history curriculum

Several history educators linked teaching an Irish dimension as part of anti-racist/multicultural history from the 1980s (Goalen, 1988; Swift, 1986), especially focusing on the secondary curriculum. However, since the late 1990s, its place in the primary history curriculum has been the focus of several studies. In 1996, Claire's landmark study *Reclaiming our Pasts: Equality and Diversity in the Primary History Curriculum,* provided substantial references to an Irish dimension as part of a wider consideration of diversity.

This has subsequently been referred to by Harnet and Whitehouse (2013) and this author (Bracey, 2008, 2010; Bracey et al., 2017).

Since the 1970s an Irish dimension has featured in developments related to the secondary curriculum. The Schools History Project introduced a Modern World Study called the Irish Question at Key Stage 4. Migration to Britain, which includes Irish migration, is currently a significant feature in several GCSE examination courses, although it was present in some syllabi from the 1980s. An Irish dimension has also featured in primary National Curriculum. For example, the National Curriculum in 2000 (DfEE/ QCA, 1999) specified teaching ethnic and cultural diversity together with 'aspects of the histories of England, Irelands Scotland and Wales where appropriate', although this requirement was somewhat vague to say the least. The current National Curriculum 2014 (DfE, 2013) is less specific and refers to 'the diversity of societies and relationships between different groups, as well as their own identity and challenges of their time' as a purpose of study. However, it does not explicitly refer to diversity else-where, subsuming it into the second order concept similarity and difference. The document includes reference to 'these islands' in its aims but this is not fully reflected in the list of statutory or non-statutory content. The only reference to Ireland is the Scots invasion at Key Stage 2. A report for the Runnymede Trust drew attention to the way in which diversity was provided for in the National Curriculum:

> There is less explicit emphasis on racial and ethnic diversity, particularly within Britain itself. Whilst the previous curriculum included a stated focus on diverse social, cultural, and religious identities, the new curriculum downplays the internal diverse histories of 'our Island story', placing them as 'out there' rather than 'in here' and of relevance 'then' rather than 'now'.
>
> (Alexander et al., 2015)

Moncrieffe (2018) drew particular attention to the implications of the structure of the National Cur-riculum with respect to teaching for diversity in the primary school history curriculum:

> The national curriculum for key stage 2 history stops at the year 1066. It provides no other significant narrative of mass-migration and settlement to the British Isles for children to learn of. It is framed by Euro-centric perspectives of 'nation building' and 'national identity'. Here is how a statutory national policy directive for teaching and learning in schools can 'whitewash' and 'erase' broader ethnic and multicultural histories.
>
> (Moncrieffe, 2018)

However, teachers as 'agents' of change can address this issue by building a curriculum which is underpinned by diversity, together with disciplinary requirements such as teaching a coherent understanding of the 'long arc of the past'. It is necessary to appreciate that the statutory content requirements are limited and need to be related to a broadly based understanding of the past. This provides significant scope for developing an Irish dimension within the primary history curriculum.

REFLECTION

How does an Irish dimension relate to teaching diversity in the primary history curriculum?

Could some of these considerations apply to other non-visible communities within our society, such as gypsy and travellers, or migrants from Eastern Europe?

What are the planning implications for an Irish dimension?

The following threads provide a framework for developing an understanding of Ireland's past and its relationship with recent and contemporary events. They will be followed by a consideration of how primary history can contribute to this framework.

1. **Ireland from earliest times in the context of 'these islands'.**

2. **Relations between England and Ireland since 1066.**

3. **Ireland from the 1970s to the present day.**

The first focus is particularly relevant to Key Stage 2 and contributes to a broadly based understanding of the past. The second and third foci relate more explicitly to work which can be undertaken in secondary school. However, the second can provide a context for topics undertaken at Key Stage 1 and Key Stage 2, provided the content and approach used relate to the need of the children. As such it compares with other sensitive and controversial topics related to diversity such as the Holocaust and slavery. The third focus needs to be set in the hinterland provided by the first and second points. The complex and sensitive nature of the recent past is usually more appropriate for secondary age pupils. However, to avoid using the past simply to address recent and contemporary issues it needs to build on a broadly based understanding of the past. Lee and Shemilt (2007) have argued that using history to address human rights issues is at odds with developing an understanding of the past. They argue that the history curriculum should provide a broadly based understanding of the past, creating a context for considering current issues. The study of Ireland as part of this broader understanding of the past in both primary as well as secondary history provides an appropriate context for understanding what is happening today.

How can an Irish dimension contribute to primary children's understanding of the past?

This section will demonstrate how the three points raised in the previous section can be related to the primary curriculum. The primary curriculum at Key Stage 1 provides opportunities to include an Irish dimension from the recent to distant past, local history, together with significant people such as Grace O' Malley, Saint Brendan, or St Columba, alongside figures from other cultures. At Key Stage 2 there are opportunities for including it within topics related to local history, the period before 1066, as well as topics related to the period since 1066.

Ireland from earliest times in the context of 'these islands'

The primary history curriculum at Key Stage 2 provides a particular opportunity for developing an awareness of an Irish dimension as part of 'these islands' before 1066 (Bracey, 2021). A study of pre-historic times which focuses on Stonehenge gives children the impression that people only lived in southern Britain. This can be addressed by using pictures from elsewhere in 'these islands', such as Carrowmore tomb in Ireland. Roman occupation was restricted to southern Britain, but Tacitus wrote that Agricola, the Roman general responsible for much of the Roman conquest of Britain, 'saw that Ireland...conveniently situated for the ports of Gaul might prove a valuable acquisition'. This was never carried out which raises questions such as – why did the Romans invade southern Britain but not Ireland? After the collapse of Roman rule, there is evidence of invasions from Ireland to western parts of Britain. However, of greater importance was the spread of the Celtic Church, associated with Ireland's 'Golden Age of Learning'. St Columba and missionaries brought the Celtic Church to northern Britain establishing religious centres at Iona and Lindisfarne. By studying the spread of the Celtic Church it is possible to see how it came to be seen as a challenge to the Roman Church in the build up to the Synod of Whitby. The impact of the Vikings on these islands was particularly evident in southern Britain and Ireland. A comparison between Dublin and Yorvik provides an appreciation of their impact on trade. However, whereas both areas suffered raids and fought the Vikings there were differences between them. This can be exemplified through looking at Alfred the Great in England and Brian Boru in Ireland. In England the Vikings and Saxons clashed over control of the land while the wars helped promote the growing power of Alfred and his successors. In Ireland the Vikings eventually became integrated in local rivalry between rival kings, which was reflected in a famous battle at Clontarf in 1014 involving Brian Boru (Gove-Humphries et al., 2013; Bracey, 2021) (Figure 8.1).

Overall, an Irish dimension for the period before 1066 contributes to a more nuanced understanding of 'these islands' which could be related to any school context. However, the following teacher demonstrated how they related an Irish dimension to the particular context of their school.

Figure 8.1   An engraving Brian Boru

Case study 1

This teacher taught in Cornwall where the Romans, Saxons and Vikings had less impact on this area than most parts of England. Consequently, they made the following rationale for including an Irish dimension:

> *I think it would be very wrong of the children to think … Cornwall sits on its own … I want them to realise that you have Brittany, Wales, Ireland, and Scotland, and how these counties have a similar background …. So, I think it is incredibly important not to think that 'We are special on our own' and there is that multicultural aspect.*

Relations between England and Ireland since 1066

The English conquest of Ireland took place from the 12th century, but there was a significant change with the Protestant Plantations from the time of Elizabeth I. Ireland was merged into Great Britain between the Acts of Union in 1801 and the founding of the Republic in 1922, with Northern Ireland remaining as part of Great Britain. This time span particularly relates to the Key Stage 3 history curriculum. However, an appreciation of what took place provides a contextual appreciation for some topics at Key Stage 1 or Key Stage 2. What follows will focus on how two contentious topics associated with this time span that could be related to teaching children in primary school.

The Elizabethan Plantations: The Reformation in England had led to a clash with the Catholic Church. There were fears that Catholic Ireland would offer a base for European powers such as Spain or France to invade Protestant England. Protestant Planters from England and Scotland were tasked with subduing and ruling over the native Catholic Irish population. How could you relate to this with primary children? This context provides a context for teaching Grace O' Malley at either Key Stage 1 or 2. At Key Stage 1 her story could be personalised around events in her life around the enquiry question – was Grace O' Malley a pirate? (Bracey et al., 2011; Gove-Humphries et al., 2013) (Figure 8.2).

The following case study demonstrates approaches which can be used to relate Grace's experiences with this age group:

Case study 2

A Key Stage 1 teacher working in a small village school in the Midlands.

> *I would tell the story for a bit then they [the children] would act a bit and then we would freeze frame. Then I would ask them how they felt … I still don't think that all the children really understood what life was like … so it was trying really. I chose all the best bits [of her life such as] the dinner when she wasn't let in and the kidnapping and then when she met Queen Elizabeth … even when she was in prison. I got the children to draw a picture of what they thought she looked like and [they began by drawing] cowboy jails and [we refined this by asking] what would it have been like to be in a castle …*

Figure 8.2   Statue representing Grace o' Malley, Westport House, Co. Mayo, Ireland

she wouldn't have light; she wouldn't have heat … and really got them to try and think about her experiences.

At Key Stage 2, this topic could be developed by developing an emotional timeline of her life and comparing it with the life of Elizabeth I and Mary Queen of Scots as a means of exploring their different challenges and experiences in the context of religious change.

The Famine/Hunger in mid-19th century Ireland: this event is associated with starvation and distress, and mass migration from Ireland. The extent that what happened was simply a natural disaster or connected to the policies of the British government is highly contentious. At Key Stage 2, this topic could support a nuanced understanding of the Victorian period based around the following enquiry question – Is the triumph of the Railway Age all we need to know about the Victorians? The following case study on Key Stage 2 teacher's approach to adapting the emotional and sensitive issues associate with the Famine/Hunger.

Case study 3

A teacher who undertook a cross-curricular approach to teaching the Famine/Hunger. This teacher used a historical novel called *Under the Hawthorne Tree* (Conlon-McKenna, 1982) to personalise the event and dance as a focus for learning. However, work undertaken in history lessons focused on subject-related objectives and included a comparison between rural life in Ireland with factory conditions in England. When using historical fiction there was a need to distinguish between the text and evidence from the time.

Migration to Britain from Ireland: The proximity of Ireland to Britain has meant that migration has taken place since earliest time. There are several ways in which this can be related to a broader consideration of migration and the development of our multicultural society (Bracey and Jackson, 2019). Firstly, an Irish dimension can relate to local history at Key Stage 1 or 2 based on the stories of people who have come to live in the community. Secondly, a post 1066 study of migration since 1066 should include Irish people, alongside other people who have come here (Lyndon-Cohen, 2020). Finally, an overview lesson related to migration since 1066 can be included in a study of the Romans, for example, drawing out similarities and differences between them, relating the topic to a 'long arc of the past'.

Ireland from the 1970s to the present day

This is usually more appropriate for teaching in the secondary school. However, the following case study indicates how a primary teacher related this to the ethnicity of the children in their school, as well as linking a historical topic to the recent past.

Case study 4

This teacher taught a Year 4 class in a Catholic School in an urban conurbation where 45% of the children had Irish heritage. With respect to the specific needs of children from ethic minority backgrounds she stated:

> I think it is a self-esteem thing as well. I really feel that so many children who are from minority background can't hook into a lot of aspects in the curriculum and I think it is essential that children see themselves within their learning and recognise their own people, their own names and that they have a sense of who they are and value that culture.

She took steps to both include an Irish dimension within topics where possible, including Grace O'Malley at Key Stage 1 and referring to Ireland as part of Key Stage 2 work on the Tudors, but also made links between past and more recent events.

This teacher had a particular reason for developing an Irish dimension. These principles could be applied to children from different ethnicities – whether it is related to the choice of significant people at Key Stage 1 or post 1066 migrant experiences, for example. The fundamental principle here is that children should be taught a diverse range of experiences when learning about the past.

REFLECTION

What are the implications of an Irish dimension for the history curriculum in my school? What are the implications of an Irish dimension for the history topics which I teach?

CHAPTER SUMMARY

The significance of an Irish dimension within a genuinely diverse curriculum relates to both its place in a broader understanding of 'these islands', together with ways in which it relates to an understanding of the emergence of our multicultural society. The National Curriculum provides scope for its development through the requirement to teach diversity, 'these islands' similarity and difference, the long arc of the past, or interpretations of the past but provides minimal substantive reference to an Irish dimension, or for that matter, any aspect of diversity. However, there are opportunities to develop an Irish dimension through the primary curriculum which is both appropriate to their age and contributes to diversity. Although the extent to which schools will develop an Irish dimension may vary depending on context and ethnicity of their children, its contribution to this wider understanding of diversity justifies its place within a curriculum which seeks to provide a broadly based understanding of our past.

References

Ajegbo, K., Kuwan, D. and Sharma, S. (2007) *Curriculum Review. Diversity and Citizenship*. Nottingham: Department for Education and Skills.

Alexander, C., Weekes-Bernard, D. and Chatterji, J. (2015) *History Lessons Teaching Diversity in and Through the History National Curriculum*. Runneymede Trust. Available at: **https://www.runnymedetrust.org/currentPublications/teaching-resources.html**

Bracey, P. (2008) *Perceptions of an Irish Dimension, and Its Significance for the English History Curriculum*; unpublished PhD theses. Birmingham: University of Birmingham.

Bracey, P. (2010) Perceptions of the contribution of an Irish dimension in the English history curriculum. *Educational Review, 62*(2): 203–213.

Bracey, P. (2021) Teaching 'these islands' from prehistoric times to 1066. *Primary History, 89*, pp. 12–17. (in process).

Bracey, P., Gove-Humphries, A. and Jackson, D. (2011) 'They did things differently then'– diversity and challenge from KS1. *Education 3–13, 39*(4): 373–382.

Bracey, P. and Jackson, D. (2020) Migration to Britain through time. *Primary History, 85*: 46–50.

Bracey, P., Jackson, D. and Gove-Humphries, A. (2017) Diversity and history education. In I. Davies (ed.), *Debates in History Teaching*, 2nd edition. London: Routledge, pp. 202–212.

Claire, H. (1996) *Reclaiming Our Pasts: Equality and Diversity in the Primary School*. Stoke: Trentham.

Conlon-McKenna, M. (1996) *Under the Hawthorn Tree*. Dublin: O'Brien Press.

DfE (2013) *History Programmes of Study: Key Stages 1 and 2 National Curriculum in England*. London: Crown Copyright.

DfEE/QCA (1999) *History: The National Curriculum for England Key Stages 1–3*. London: Department for Education/Qualifications and Curriculum Authority.

Goalen, P. (1988) Multiculturalism and the lower school history syllabus: towards a practical approach. *Teaching History*, *53*: 8–16.

Gove-Humphries, A., Bracey, P. and Jackson, D. (2013) 'Why are you so angry Grace?' Teaching and learning about Grace O'Malley as a significant woman at Key Stage 1. *Primary History Issue, 65*: 22–23.

Harnet, P. and Whitehouse, S. (2013) Creative exploration of local, national, and global links. In H. Cooper (ed.), *Teaching History Creatively*. London: Routledge, pp. 153–167.

Lee, P. and Shemilt, D. (2007) New alchemy or fatal attraction? History and citizenship. *Teaching History*, *129*: 14–19.

Lyndon-Cohen, D. (2020) *Primary Scheme of Work: Journeys – The Story of Migration to Britain*. Historical Association.

Moncrieffe, M.L. (2018) Teaching and learning about cross-cultural encounters over the ages through the story of Britain's migrant past. In R. Race (ed.), *Advancing Multicultural Dialogues in Education*. Cham: Palgrave Macmillan, pp. 195–214.

Parekh, B. (2000) *The Future of Multi-Ethnic Britain: The Parekh Report*. London: Profile.

Phillips, R. (1998) *History Teaching, Nationhood and the State: A Study in Educational Politics*. London: Cassell.

Swift, R. (1986) 'The Teaching of Irish History in the Secondary School.' In *Teaching History*. No. 44, pp. 16–19.

Sewell, T., Aderin-Pocock, Chughtai, A., Fraser, K., Khalid, N. and Moyo, D. (2021) *Commission on Race and Ethnic Disparities*. London: Gov.UK.

Slater, J. (1989) *The Politics of History Teaching: A Humanity Dehumanised?* Institute of Education, Special Professorial Lecture. London: Institute of Education. Cited in Phillips, R. (1998) History Teaching, Nationhood, and the State: A Study in Educational Politics, London.

9

THE DANGERS OF 'SINGLE STORIES' IN PRIMARY GEOGRAPHY EDUCATION

ANTHONY BARLOW

KEYWORDS: DISTANT PLACE; GRAPHICACY; ORIENTALISM; REACHER DEVELOPMENT; SINGLE AND BINARY STORIES; SUBSTANTIVE AND DISCIPLINARY KNOWLEDGE

CHAPTER OBJECTIVES

The aims of this chapter are:

- To recognise that all knowledge is partial and subject to revision, discussion and debate.
- To consider teaching about 'distant places' as an essential part of the primary geography curriculum.
- To discuss the responsibility of teachers when generalising and creating models and approximations to avoid stereotyping.
- To remind children that any people/place are real and that in a post-colonial United Kingdom, we might think even more carefully about how we represent multiple identities.

CCF ITE links

3.3	Ensuring pupils' master foundational concepts and knowledge before moving on is likely to build confidence and help them succeed.
3.4	Anticipating misconceptions is an important aspect of curricular knowledge.
3.5	Explicitly teaching pupils the knowledge and skills they need to succeed within particular subject areas is beneficial.

Introduction

Teaching about 'distant places' is an essential part of the primary geography curriculum. When simplifying the world for under 11s, we must generalise and create models and approximations that can lead to stereotyping. Geography is no exception in selecting elements to portray complex ideas, but as it deals with the *real world* today, it means we have an additional responsibility to consider how this reality is constructed and explained. These distant places are inhabited spaces, real people's lives and in a post-colonial United Kingdom, we should think carefully about how we represent others' identities. Teachers should tread cautiously when teaching geography, choosing sources carefully and reflecting on how they teach comparison, contrast and imagined environments similar and different to our own, recognising that our knowledge will always be partial, and subject to revision and debate.

Building and enhancing an understanding of the world and its landscapes and ecosystems is the role of a geography teacher. This starts with naming these phenomena. However, in connecting locations through a spatial framework, success will come from a deep knowledge of the location(s) being studied. For example, such a framework connects London to the South East of the country of England and to the United Kingdom. Another connects Rio de Janeiro with the country of Brazil in South America and the Southern Hemisphere. What the National Curriculum (2014) in England asks us to do is consider the character of these locations to build understanding.

It is this character of a location that is a subjective measure – what characteristics should we select, and which are of prime importance? This is what we might mean by deep description, going beyond the locational proper nouns and adding lots of further nouns and adverbs to describe these locations. In curriculum studies and academic geography, this is called 'place knowledge'. It is my contention that critical appreciation about the selection of this knowledge is essential to share, develop and explain to pupils.

Place knowledge stories

Place knowledge works best where the sometimes human and the physical binaries of the discipline are joined in narratives (or 'stories') of how things came to be and why. When these stories cohere, they merge and overlap, providing a 'sense of place' which in turn supports a pupils' development of a number of concepts in the subject. This is preferred to a view supported by atomised labels, lists, out-of-context diagrams or unconnected descriptions.

Inspiration for this chapter

Chimamanda Ngozi Adichie's 'Danger of a Single Story' 2009 TED talk is the main stimulus for this chapter. In it, Adichie considers how if we only consider *self* as opposed to an *'other'*, we lose the richness that our lives hold. As Adiche describes, we are all composed of many aspects and many overlapping stories in our lives (TED, 2009). Adichie warns that many of these stories we tell perpetuate stereotypes – they are single stories. This popular talk has resonated widely over the past decade and shaped geographical thinking including in relation to primary geography education in the United Kingdom (Barlow and Whitehouse, 2019; Biddulph, 2011; Enser, 2021; Martin, 2013; Ofsted, 2021b; Scoffham, 2018).

Single stories in geography

It is worth sharing as we begin what the focus of geography education might be. At its heart, it is about who, how and why things occur on the terrestrial and marine biomes, where **geo-** relates to the earth, and **-graphy** to writing, essentially earth-writing! Any teacher will bring coherence to the **stories** they tell if they form a picture of how the world is, how it might be and how it came to be alongside selecting their knowledge and stories carefully.

Any number of primary geography education writers have noted the usefulness of such stories to help create a sense of narrative in how children view the world (Barlow, 2017 in Catling, Ed., Tanner and Whittle, 2013; Witt, 2013). 'Earth stories' offer the potential to connect and inform, but also risk dividing and misinforming if not selected carefully enough.

Adichie suggests that single story narratives are a problem, as they often feature outdated and problematic perspectives. As teachers, if we are not thoughtful, critical and reflective about the knowledge sources (and stories) we impart, we risk passing on at best, misunderstandings about the world, and at worst, creating division between the children we teach and the world beyond. This might not just be people or locations overseas, given the diversity of many locations in the United Kingdom; this could be in relating to their own identities, to their own community or wider family.

Geography has an international perspective and the subject desires to help children develop a sense of issues beyond borders. Scoffham (2017: 1) argues, 'No other primary school subject has such a clear international focus or directly seeks to develop global understanding. It puts them into context in relationship to other people, locations and environments'.

The National Curriculum supports developing a sense of story through it desire to build a 'contextual knowledge of the location of globally significant places – both terrestrial and marine – including their defining physical and human characteristics' (DfE, 2014a: 1).

Scoffham continues that:

> other countries and cultures feature only tangentially in the history curriculum and are little more than a footnote in art and music. In other subjects the global dimension is almost completely absent. The responsibility for developing a secure framework of world knowledge and understanding is thus located firmly within the geography curriculum and is the responsibility of geography teachers.
>
> (2017: 2)

Sense of identity and stories

Adichie talks powerfully about her early life in Nigeria, where her world was based on what she experienced as part of a middle-class Nigerian family. The rest of the world was seen in the books that she read. As someone who had never been outside Nigeria, she says: 'We didn't have snow, we ate mangoes, and we never talked about the weather, because there was no need to [and] … the characters in the British books I read drank ginger beer. Never mind that I had no idea what ginger beer was' (Adichie, 2009).

She continues remarking about stories' power: we are all impressionable and vulnerable in the face of a story, 'particularly as children. Because all I had read were books in which characters were foreign, I had become convinced that books by their very nature had to have foreigners in them and had to be about things with which I could not personally identify. Now, things changed when I discovered African books' (Adichie, 2009).

Adichie's identity developed still further when she travelled outside the continent of her birth being shocked in the United States as she didn't up until this point consciously identify as African. Her story was simplified to relate to the continent as a whole rather than an individual nation so, 'in the U.S., whenever Africa came up, people turned to me. Never mind that I knew nothing about places like Namibia. But I did come to embrace this new identity, and in many ways I think of myself now as African' (Adichie, 2009).

Stories without boundaries or binaries

To compound the issue of 'self' and 'other' there also exists the binary of human and physical geography that splits the world into 'us and the natural world'. This has been promoted through the national curriculum's lists and bullet points which show human and then physical aspects/labels in its headings. New or inexperienced teachers may feel the need to approach these two elements of the subject separately instead of mutually dependant. Stewart (2014) suggests this '20th century' schism should be removed. This distinction is indeed no longer promoted within the Early Years Framework (2021) as elements within the aspect of understanding the world are seen as more inter-related.

It is points of commonality and interdisciplinarily, a consideration of the whole rather than just parts that we need to build in our stories. This links well with the current Ofsted focus in schools in England to make sure that all curricula are well-sequenced, building on what has gone before (2021a). Indeed, the Ofsted Research Review comments that it is through fieldwork, in particular that we can draw together pupils' locational knowledge and that of human and physical processes as 'it supports pupils to appreciate the interplay between them' (2021b). Difficulties arise when fieldwork is not available, and there are few materials to support the busy teacher.

Fieldwork is a good example of where geography teaching has the power to support a child's connections to the world. It allows them to feel at home or their place in it and gain a sense of scale, a key geographical concept. We want them to make stories for the future as well, so when they see something, they can start to wonder and think *why* or *how could it be different*?

If stories are overlapping, then children can match their experience against other views or other sources they might have been taught. It is, in the words of R.S. Peters from 1965, possible that children can then travel like a geographer and with 'a different view'. This was borrowed for the 2009 Geographical Association Manifesto for geography and forms a strong intent and implementation plan for the power of telling geographical stories.

Identity: how we see ourselves is important

Identity has been the subject of much debate in recent years. So-called fundamental 'British Values' are said to be democracy, the rule of law, individual liberty, and mutual respect and tolerance for those of different faiths and beliefs (DfE, 2014a).

REFLECTION

Think about how you see yourself and where you 'fit in'. This will be related to where you live, who is in your community, who you come into contact with, what media you consume. What has made your identity? Fran Martin in her Geographical Association Conference address in 2012 said that she is a member of these groups among others: twin, boogie boarder, member of LGBT community, primary geographer and global citizen (Martin, 2012).

Identity and children's ideas

All representations of place require simplification; you can never get a 'whole picture'. So, often, and this is Adichie's contention, some parts of the world might be see in a positive light, while others might be seen in a negative one or be portrayed as afflicted by war, natural and human disasters (Scoffham, 2017). Wiegand (1992) considers Piaget and Weill's (1951) contention that children's ideas of *others* in their *homeland* and *distant place* are the result of a 'complex relationship between development in the cognitive and affective domains' (1992: 36). He goes on to discuss the idea of reciprocity as being important the ability to 'look at the world from someone else's point of view'.

Martin and Griffiths (2014) consider a relational logic when understanding pupils' personal geographies which leads to a more open-minded, non-judgemental stance towards difference. From this perspective, culture and identity are understood through relating to difference, and as dynamic, fluid and plural (Brah, 2007, cited in Martin and Griffiths, 2014). Martin describes this as 'relational thinking', where difference is seen as a relation rather than a distinction' (Martin, 2013: 410).

How might difference be taught?

Walker suggests that children in English schools have 'existing, and probably muddled, fleeting and improbable ideas about unfamiliar places; there exists potential for teachers to challenge these perceptions towards more clear, stable and probable ideas' (2004: 1). Most distant places tend to be seen in terms of facts and figures, rather than a rich and complicated interplay of people and their environment (Grigg and Hughes, 2013).

Using our own stories

Should we use our own experiences of travel to teach? This is always a difficult conundrum. You visited Kenya on safari, drove the coastal route from Cape Town and had a city-break to Morocco: do you know Africa? Obviously not, but you do have three points of contrast from North and South in the continent. You can then start to piece together what might be in-between. Neiman quoting George Santayana says 'all tourists are dear to Hermes, the god of travel, who is patron also of amiable curiosity and freedom of mind. There is wisdom in turning as often as possible from the familiar to the unfamiliar: it keeps the mind nimble, it kills prejudice, and it fosters humour' (Santayana in Neiman, 2016: 158). So, building on this 'amiable curiosity' we can also foster creativity and creative thinking.

REFLECTION

Can you think of how you could use your own experiences of travel to promote children's curiosity about the world not yet seen?

Comparing us and the other: orientalism

No man is an island, Entire of itself; Each is a piece of the Continent, A part of the main.

(John Donne)

Adichie started to develop a whole new set of stories as she reflected on her childhood, on her life in Nigeria and then built new ones when she met new people. With children we need to support a recognition of their story, of who they are and their own sense of identity. Knowing where our story sits in relationship to others is important as we start to consider the teaching of geography. We are all connected, as poet Donne (1572–1631) suggests in the quote. We all hold values and attitudes about the world, as will the children we teach, and this can have an impact on our ability to teach.

Casting other people as 'others' in our stories, Said (1999) suggests, reminds us that, just like Adichie until her view of herself is challenged by meeting new people, most people are principally aware of one culture, setting and home. This is not the same for those who have moved from one place to another to live. He goes on to say that 'exiles are aware of at least two, and this plurality of vision gives rise to an awareness of simultaneous dimensions…For an exile, habits of life, expression, or activity in the new environment inevitably occur against the memory of these things in another environment.'

(Said, 2013: 186, Online)

REFLECTION

Consider the word *exile*. Like when teaching distant place – everywhere is distant until you go there and experience it – do you consider yourself an exile? Do you teach chidren who might be exiles, having family or connections to other locations in the world? Said says that all cultures spin out a story of self and other, where you are native, authentic and the other is foreign and perhaps threatening. 'From this dialectic comes the series of heroes and monsters, founding fathers and barbarians, prized masterpieces and despised opponents that express a culture from its deepest sense of national self-identity to its refined patriotism, and finally to its coarse jingoism, xeno-phobia, and exclusivist bias' (Said, 1999: 40).

Consider this in relation to who you know and how you consider others. Consider in relation to how you have felt before you have gone to some 'foreign' part of the country or nation.

Said's writing on the geographies of 'self' and 'other' show an interplay between power, knowledge and representation. Geography in the primary school might be a corrective to this. It could be said that globalisation might give us an impression of knowing other people and locations better than we do. We all know the shock of going somewhere new and thinking, *'I can't believe it works like that here!'*. Bear in mind that when considering using your own travel experiences that it is at least as important for learning about yourself, and reflecting back on your own culture, as it is for under-standing others.

Knowledge and the other

The current English schools' geography National Curriculum (2014) can suggest that geography is about a checklist of elements of subject knowledge to be mastered. This 'knowledge turn' (Lambert, 2011) is promoted by Ofsted with the focus firmly on 'knowing more and remembering more' (2019). In creating an emphasis on teachers imparting knowledge, there is a danger that working to draw nuances of knowing of and from others can be lost.

Materials we use

Geographers use familiar media (such as maps, images, books and video) and this allows us to see the wonders of the world beyond and to try comprehend what it is might be like in someone else's shoes, to see what they see or what it would be like to live *there*. We use, in Massey's coinage, our *geographical imaginations* (2006). Any children that we teach geography need to have their imaginations sparked, but also a 'critical graphicacy' must be developed alongside this. This will allow them to develop and challenge stereotypical views. In order to do this the contrasts they see must be as accurate as possible. Our challenge as teachers is to consider the sourcing of such materials and think through the pitfalls that might occur if we do not do this sensitively.

Critical graphicacy

Graphicacy is said to be the 'fourth ace in the pack' (Balchin and Coleman, 1966) of essential skills in geography. 'Graphicacy can be thought of as the sub-set of visual-spatial thinking that applies particularly to geography. It refers to the essentially pictorial ways, from photographs to diagrams and maps, in which we communicate spatial information about places, spaces and environments. Its most refined form is, perhaps, the OS map with its distinctive style and conventions, e.g. plan view, symbols and contours' (Mackintosh, 2011: 7). Critical graphicacy allows children to question the visual sources rather than accept them at face value. If not used judiciously, resources can detach us from individual stories, connections and an understanding of how an individual, family or community might live where we are studying.

REFLECTION

Consider what impression you gain from using maps and tourism material in relation to where you are located. Try it – search for where you live and see if it is your lived experience which the internet serves up.

Stories we should be careful how we tell

Numerical data are also an important source for geographers. These, however, need to be put into context rather than just memorised in isolation. As teachers, we need to have a sense of proportion: how much of the world are we referring to when we consider individual case studies?

A sense of scale in your stories is important

Consider the following statistics, and then think about the story that you have or tell of where you live compared to other places.

1.9 million in Northern Ireland 3 million in Wales 5.5 million in Scotland 9 million in London	**67 million in the United Kingdom**	**7.7 billion in the world**

Did any of these surprise you? Can you even imagine what a million people is like, never mind a billion?

Now consider the context in which you live and teach and consider it in relation to these questions.

Where you live	Consider				
A village	Where you live in relation to the centre. Do you feel like you live in the centre or edge (suburbs)?	Is it located on a river, a main road or transport route?	Is it here because of an industry of a particular	How close to the coast are you? Where is your nearest major source of fresh water?	How high up are you? What can you see from this viewpoint?
A small town					
A large town					
A city					

Examples of good practice: case studies

Teaching distant places

As has been suggested, case studies of real locations, people and environments might be best used to teach children about distant and unfamiliar places. This is a familiar teaching approach and allows us to present images and ideas to match, and challenge children's initial ideas so that reconsider them. Images to develop graphicacy should be at the core of place studies in class-based tasks.

Developing great stories with children through rich case studies

Individuals' stories:	Media for children:
An individual only ever has themselves to draw upon, so if used alongside image sets, maps and video materials, where they can show comparison and contrast this is a valuable form of representing a location.	BBC Teach (via You Tube) and BBC Bitesize have powerful stories with children, saying how their lives are. Examples are the Class Clips series **https://www.bbc.co.uk/teach/class-clips-video/geography-a-child-led-tour-of-kinderdijk-in-the-netherlands/zrpyrj6**
While never representative of a wider view, using guest speakers can enliven the rest of your pupils' learning about the human and physical geography of a location.	**Media for adults:**
	Many BBC documentaries are split into ten-minute segments, and examples from authored documentaries from, for example, David Attenborough or Simon Reeve alongside series like Earth's Great Rivers or even CountrFile, Springwatch and BBC News can provide just enough stimulus to create a fascinating conversation about how a landscape came to be. If the soundtrack is too distracting or complex, turn the sound off.
If they have photos of their life, travels and opinion on the country, it can broaden this out and not remain just one story.	

Books: There are coffee table books on almost every country, region or city in the world. One series I like is the Dorling Kindersley *Children Just Like* series (DK/Penguin/Random House, 2016) and *Food Like Mine* (Children Just Like Me) (DK, 2017). An outstanding Key Stage 1 series of books focuses on individual countries.The *World Alphabets* series includes titles such as Ifeoma Onyefulu's A is for Africa (1997) et al. (Frances Lincoln), R is for Russia (2011) etc.

Considering landmarks

Do we ever critically evaluate urban areas and cities? How do we present landmark buildings to children: is it always with a sense of 'wow'? Would you want to live in a big building's shadow? Do you know buildings like this cause an increase in winds below and around them? Imagine if London was seen as just the high buildings. What relationship do these have on the daily lives of nine million Londoners?

Just considering the single story of cities as being what is above ground ignore the magnificent structures underground as well as the physical geography that the city is built on. What is Manhattan Island in New York, if we don't discuss it being an island situated in the mouth of the Hudson River which empties here into New York Bay and the Atlantic Ocean? This is one of the largest natural harbours in the world, but do we teach this? Should we portray this story too? The physical location of the place shapes the lives of the people as well.

REFLECTION

Think of any major world cities whether you have been to them or not. Look on their internet (Wikipedia or online encyclopaedia entry) profile and consider the description of their geography. Did you realise this when you visited? Did you notice that there were lots of hills (Rome, Edinburgh, Moscow, San Francisco), it was by a lake or the sea (Chicago, Barcelona and Cape Town) or that they were very flat (Las Vegas, a hot desert) or surrounded by hills with a river running through it (Paris and many European cities).

Final thought: geography without a sense of deficit

One key concept mentioned at the outset in this chapter is developing 'sense of place' (Massey, 1994) where regions are created by 'drawing lines around a place' and so defining it but this can fossilise a location. Massey seeks a progressive sense of place where 'it is absolutely not static', and it could almost be called a 'process' because of this change (1994: 7, 8).

We need to recognise that so much of the African continent has changed from what it might have been even ten years ago and a number of writers talk of the problem of having a charity mentality in relation to people in different countries (e.g. Simpson, 2017; Scoffham, 2018). As Adichie says: 'when I left Nigeria to go to university in the United States, I was 19. My American roommate was shocked by me. She asked where I had learned to speak English so well…She asked if she could listen to what she called my "tribal music", and was consequently very disappointed when I produced my tape of Mariah Carey. She assumed that I did not know how to use a stove. What struck me was this: She had felt sorry for me even before she saw me. Her default position toward me, as an African, was a kind of patronizing, well-meaning pity. My roommate had a single story of Africa: a single story of catastrophe. In this single story, there was no possibility of Africans being similar to her in any way, no possibility of feelings more complex than pity, no possibility of a connection as human equals' (Adiche, 2009).

CHAPTER SUMMARY

In this chapter, I have shown the importance of building and enhancing your geography curriculum from the substantive knowledge that comes from knowing where somewhere is and then enhancing this knowledge by developing a deep sense of place knowledge. Keep in mind the subjectivity of this and that place knowledge works best where the locational. Human and the physical binaries of the discipline should be joined in narratives to build on stories they already know. A scoped and sequenced curriculum is of vital importance. When the stories cohere, merge and overlap, they support pupils' development of geography concepts such as place, space, scale and cultural identities. While sometimes these aspects might be beyond our knowing, we need to make sure we consider common pitfalls when understanding others.

Further reading

@EYPPC_GA runs regular free CPD events under the banner GeogLive See the online support sessions here: **https://www.youtube.com/channel/UCgzLz6CzszzDS1xZIf3ZqzQ**.

Adichie, C. (2009) *The Danger of a Single Story*. TED Conferences. Available at: **https://www.ted.com/talks/chimamanda_ngozi_adichie_the_danger_of_a_single_story** (Last accessed 20 April 2022).

Barlow, A. and Whitehouse, S. (2019) *Mastering Primary Geography*. London: Bloomsbury.

Catling, S. and Martin, F. (2011) Contesting powerful knowledge: the primary geography curriculum as an articulation between academic and children's (ethno-). *Geographies Curriculum Journal, 22*(3): 317–335.

Pirbhai-Illich, F., Pete, S. and Martin, F. (2017) *Culturally Responsive Pedagogy: Working towards Decolonization, Indigeneity and Interculturalism*. London: Springer.

RGS-IBG (2017) *Chair's Theme: Decolonising Geographical Knowledges: Opening Geography Out to the World RGS-IBG Annual Conference, 2017, London*. https://rgs-ibg.onlinelibrary.wiley.com/doi/abs/10.1111/area.12371 (accessed, 20 April 2022).

Scoffham, S. and Owens, P. (2017) *Blooomsbury Curriculum Basics: Geography*. London: Bloomsbury.

Willy, T. (2020) *Leading Primary Geography*. Sheffield: Geographical Association. Available at: **https://geognc.wordpress.com/**

Witt, S. (2020) Paying attention to a more-than-human world. *Primary Geography: Autumn 2020, 103*: 12–13, Sheffield: Geographical Association.

References

Balchin, W.G.V. and Coleman, A.M. (1966) Cartographica. *The International Journal for Geographic Information and Geovisualization, 3*(1): 23–28.

Barlow, A. (2017) *Reflections on Primary Geography*. Blackheath: Register of Research in Primary Geography. Local ways into ESD: Wonder-ful thinking at the dump.

Biddulph, M. (2011) Editorial: the danger of a single story. *Teaching Geography, 36*(2): 45.

DfE (2014a) *Promoting Fundamental British Values Through SMSC*. Available at: **https://www.gov.uk/government/publications/promoting-fundamental-british-values-through-smsc** (accessed 20 April 2022)

DfE (2014b) *The National Curriculum in England: Complete Framework for Key Stages 1 to 4*. Available at: **https://www.gov.uk/government/publications/national-curriculum-in-england-framework-for-key-stages-1-to-4** (accessed 11 March 2019)

DfE (2021) *Statutory Framework for the Early Years Foundation Stage*. Available at: **https://www.gov.uk/government/publications/early-years-foundation-stage-framework–2** (accessed 20 April 2022)

Enser, M. (2021) *Powerful Geography: A Curriculum With Purpose in Practice*. Carmarthen: Crown House Publishing.

Geograhical Association (2009) *A Different View*. Available at: **https://www.geography.org.uk/write/MediaUploads/Support%20and%20guidance/GA_ADVBookletFULL.pdf** (Last accessed 20 April 2022).

Grigg, R. and Hughes, S. (2013) *Teaching Primary Humanities*. London: Pearson.

Lambert (2011) Reviewing the case for geography, and the 'knowledge turn' in the English National Curriculum, *The Curriculum Journal*, *22*(2): 243–264. **https://doi.org/10.1080/09585176.2011.574991**

Mackintosh, M. (2011) *Graphicacy for Life Primary Geography*. *Vol. 75*. Sheffield: Geographical Association, pp. 6–8.

Martin, F. (2012) The geographies of difference. *Geography*, *97*(3): 116–122. **https://doi.org/10.1080/00167487.2012.12094349**

Martin, F. (2013) Same old story: the problem of object-based thinking as a basis for teaching distant places. *Education 3–13*, *41*(4): 410–424. **https://doi.org/10.1080/03004279.2013.819619**

Martin, F. and Griffiths, H. (2014) Relating to the 'other': transformative, intercultural learning in post-colonial contexts compare. *A Journal of Comparative and International Education*, *44*(6): 938–959.

Massey, D. (1994) *A Global Sense of Place*. Available at: **http://aughty.org/pdf/global_sense_place.pdf**

Massey, D. (2006) The geographical mind. In D. Balderston (ed.), *Secondary Geography Handbook*. Sheffield: Geographical Association.

Neiman, S. (2016) *Why Grow Up*. London: Penguin.

Ofsted (2019) *School Inspection Update*. Available at: **https://assets.publishing.service.gov.uk/government/uploads/system/uploads/attachment_data/file/772056/School_inspection_update_-_January_2019_Special_Edition_180119.pdf** (accessed 20 April 2022)

Ofsted (2021a) *Education Inspection Framework*. Available at: **https://www.gov.uk/government/publications/education-inspection-framework/education-inspection-framework#what-inspectors-will-consider-when-making-judgements** (accessed 20 April 2022)

Ofsted (2021b) *Research Review Series: Geography*. Available at: **https://www.gov.uk/government/publications/research-review-series-geography/research-review-series-geography** (accessed 20 April 2022)

Said, E. (1999) *Out of Place*. London: Granta.

Said, E. (2013) *'Reflections on Exile', in Reflections on Exile and Other Essays*. Cambridge, MA: Harvard University Press.

Scoffham, S. (2017) *Young Children's Ideas of Different Nations, Peoples and Cultures: A Research Perspective*. Available at: **https://repository.canterbury.ac.uk/item/881q1/young-children-s-ideas-of-different-nations-peoples-and-cultures-a-research-perspective** (accessed 20 April 2022)

Scoffham, S. (2018) Global learning: a catalyst for curriculum change. *International Journal of Development Education and Global Learning*, *10*(2): 135–146.

Simpson, J. (2017) 'Learning to unlearn' the charity mentality within schools. *Policy and Practice: A Development Education Review*, *25*: 88–108.

Stewart, I. (2014) *From Geo-education to Geocommunication: New Rules of Engagement Geographical Association Conference 2014.* **https://www.youtube.com/watch?v=UA8-03pr3Rc** (accessed 20 April 2022)

Tanner, J. and Whittle, J. (2013) *The Everyday Guide to Primary Geography: Story.* Sheffield: Geographical Association.

TED (2009) Available at: **https://www.ted.com/talks/chimamanda_ngozi_adichie_the_ danger_of_a_single_story**

Wiegand, P. (1992) *Places in the Primary School.* Abingdon: Routledge.

Walker, G. (2004) Urban children's perceptions of rural villages in England (2). In S. Catling and F. Martin (eds), *Researching Primary Geography.* Special Publication No 1. pp93–106. Blackheath: Register of Research in Primary Geography Education. Available at: **https://www.geography.org.uk/ write/MediaUploads/research%20library/GA_EYPPRRActionResearch3Walker2.pdf**

Witt, S. (2013) *It's a Small World; Playful Possibilities to Explore the Geographical Concept of Place.* Conference Presentation: Geographical Association. Available at: **https://www.geography.org.uk/ download/GA_conf13Itsasmallworldpresentation.pdf**

10
PRIMARY PHYSICAL EDUCATION AND ITS COMPLEX PUZZLE OF DIVERSITY

SARAH ADAMS AND ALISON MURRAY

KEYWORDS: COLLECTIVE COMMUNITY IDENTITY; DEVELOPMENTALLY APPROPRIATE PRACTICE; EMBODIED; INTERSECTIONALITY; STRUCTURED AUTONOMY; STRUCTURED CHOICE

CHAPTER OBJECTIVES

The aims of this chapter are:

- To embody notions of constraints through a culturally holistic perspective considering the intersectionality of class members.
- To promote awareness of socially just physical education (PE) using structured choice to inform practice.

CCF ITE links

5.3	Adapting teaching in a responsive way, including by providing targeted support to pupils who are struggling, is likely to increase pupil success.

(Continued)

(Continued)

7.6	Pupils are motivated by intrinsic factors (related to their identity and values) and extrinsic factors (related to reward).
7.7	Pupils' investment in learning is also driven by their prior experiences and perceptions of success and failure.
8.2	Reflective practice, supported by feedback from and observation of experienced colleagues, professional debate, and learning from educational research, is also likely to support improvement.

Introduction

With increasing trends in migration, choice and sense of place, the world, in all its diversity, is more connected. Walking down the street, it is not unusual to hear a cacophony of different accents, languages and hear a dancing harmony of tone and colour. The need to be heard and celebrated and to be valued, in society, is a fundamental right. From a diversity perspective, the (physical) education classroom mirrors the outside world. Children arrive with energising enthusiasm to move and learn. With its nature as an embodied subject, PE plays a pivotal role in revealing and reducing barriers to encourage and support a love and means for physical engagement as a lifelong activity. However, with aspirational goals to support each and every child, will the extent of our awareness support such an objective? To recognise and celebrate the diverse wealth of individuals, we need to become and remain aware of the collective sensibilities.

Positive regard of self and others bolsters identity. Social identity is a complex phenomenon. The social construction of who we are through a collective societal standpoint evolves, and this state of flux (Korostelina, 2007) provides a living platform for our reciprocal experiences through movement education. Giddens notes identity needs to be 'routinely created and sustained in the reflective activities of the individual' (1991: 53). Our chapter seeks to provide a means for invested educational stakeholders to integrate reflective and reflexive opportunities for pupils within their teaching. It fuses ways of thinking using ethical reasoning through a meta-awareness of diversity. It opens contemplation and conversation around the interconnections of the individual with and through a collective community identity. Social identity through PE creates a marvellous opportunity to transcend Core Content Framework (CCF) enactment.

Bringing identity and diversity into education

As individuals, we are unique, influenced by motivations and lived experiences. An individual is made up of intersectionality, gender, social class, ethnicity, culture, religion and ability, for example. All these segments come together like a puzzle and contribute to an individual's sense of self and emergent identity. The puzzle pieces are not uniform, some segments are larger and more prominent than others indicating the significant role they may play in one's life. The United Kingdom is an ethnically diverse country (ONS, 2019); hence, it embraces multitudes of differing puzzles. For example, one pupil might have a puzzle composed of pieces that help shape identity, inclusive of embracing Asian, heterosexual, cisgendered female and ADHD as contributory elements. Such intersectionality and these contributing segments might be perceived through the linear analysis of privilege or disadvantage. The factor of ADHD, a large piece in this identity puzzle, could factor into the latter. What of your own factors and how these mitigate your positions, perceptions and ultimately, your practice?

REFLECTION

Think about engaging and inclusive ways your class can create and explore their collective class identity puzzle. How might this be enacted across the PE curriculum, e.g. through choices of activities in cultural dance or games, for instance?

Our own factors therefore contribute to the potential and propensity to engage, achieve, enjoy and ultimately learn. It is beholden then that our PE curriculum, and the way in which it is enacted, endorses and reflects our class identity puzzle beyond what is assumed through the limitations of the teacher's respective lived experience.

Diversity is complex. Internal and external dimensions of diversity share who we are as indicated through our ways of being and through different lenses; some more observable than others. Educators are committed to create and enact practice to bridge the intent, implementation and impact of the core context framework as embodied through a PE that is recognised by and reflective of everyone. Quality education is a child's right (UNICEF, 1989) with every child given the right to grow up in a safe and secure and nurturing environment. This can be enacted through engaging and developmentally appropriate education.

Diversity in the developmentally appropriate PE curriculum

Developmental principles in PE demand that children's bespoke pace of understanding and developing motor competence are understood and integrated as part of a dynamic and reflexive pedagogy (Graham et al., 2020). Such developmental progression facilitates a healthy and active lifelong lifestyle. PE encompasses child development as it embraces childhood, crosses adolescence and prepares young adults for a healthy active life across fundamental and sport-specific motor phases (Gabbard, 2021). Developmentally appropriate practice, using fundamental skills and movement concepts, and applied through a meaningful co-constructed curriculum provides the necessary competence children need to enter and successfully exit Early Years physical domain (DfE, 2021) and our PE National cCurriculum (DfE, 2013).

When we embody a comprehensive sense of development, we can explore the nuances around educational growth through psychomotor, cognitive, affective and well-being dimensions (or domains). The explicit addition and use of a culturally contextual dimension will inform and model to all stakeholders; that indeed, this approach is a respected and a vital part of the makeup of the PE planning and implementation experience. When learning embodies class cultural context, when all components of the class identity puzzle are identified, confirmed and affirmed, the learning becomes meaningful to all.

Explicating and embodying diversity as a pillar of the curriculum provides a means for everyone to be seen and heard. It necessitates a strategy awareness, to ensure that regardless of what we do and who we are, and our own puzzle make up, we have considered it from other perspectives. Our class identity puzzle is now a living part of our curriculum.

PE invites holistic thinking across the complexities of its planning and implementation (Ovens et al. 2008). PE has the capacity to build social relationships across culture, ethnicity and gender, uniting children in class together through the joy of learning through physical activity. Now more than ever it is imperative that our curriculum reflects the needs and aspirations of all of our learners in ways which are contextually relevant to them. By adopting a diversity lens with a focus on socially just primary PE, we empower children and teachers alike, and we provide opportunities for all members of the class community to feel appreciated, considered and valued. Contextual cultural consideration costs nothing. Rather it requires selfless and sustained thought to anticipate and respond to the known and emerging needs across the educational cycle. We contemplate such notions using and fusing constraints in part informed through pupil identity puzzles. These known and emerging factors we can use to the advantage of the class. Beyond PE, let's think bigger. For example, an elephant may not perceive barriers unless asked to try to fit into a mouse hole. The elephant would not choose that option and could just as easily feel valued and respected for its size as the mice go in one hole and the elephants a nearby entrance of a differing size. Indeed, one cave size eliminates this barrier. Likewise, the task of jumping over hurdles would not be relevant for a wheelchair user and it is important to consider an alternative task in order to challenge and inspire that learner. The hurdle task, while it is relevant for some, is clearly contextually irrelevant for others. By adopting a diversity lens through the class identity puzzle, the mouse and the elephant ought to be engaged and challenged in ways they find meaningful, at the same time, in the same space. What of constraints less obvious or not identified as potential barriers to learning.

The ecology of PE diversity and unpacking this constraint by constraint, puzzle by puzzle

Ecologically the myriad of factors around diversity through PE can be contemplated through concepts of space, effort and relationships. Opportunities which are relevant and accessible for children to develop space awareness in meaningful ways are essential. The way we move is also influenced by a myriad of factors, not least our structural and functional constraints.

Diversity, of which educators and students are a part, Ryan et al. acknowledge as multidimensional (2020). The British Council concede its complexity and commit to wholehearted embracing of 'policies and practices of equality, diversity and inclusion' (2022: 7) across all aspects of their operations. For many reasons as regards diversity, PE participation is complex (Thorjussen and Sisjord, 2018). It involves participation of the self, and that self is identity and everything therein. Learning is non-linear, adding to the complexity.

Educators and their pupils, when they embody their movement culture, develop competencies, knowledge and awareness and values around life enhancing physical activity. This journey will look and sound and feel different for all. Learning is identified as non-linear and, as such, warrants and welcomes the embodiment of such notions across the intent, implementation and reflective impact cycle through the CCF (DfE, 2019). In discerning the nonlinearity of learning, we acknowledge and appreciate that children differ in how they think, how they feel, how they move and so learn. Applying developmentally appropriate principles to PE planning and teaching ensures the pedagogical space for socially just practice. Moreover, a means to become aware of class lived constraints and perceptions from could be one means to support and sustain such ecological practice. Socially just PE embraces a conscious awareness of diversity.

One fundamental skill focused framework, set through constraints principles (Newell, 1986), provides a map as it were, for all actively involved stakeholders, the pupils and educators, to use the constraints they perceive around them (Murray and Kaitell, 2022). To do so, the learner, the environment of learning and educator are collectively considered (Jia-Yi Chow et al., 2012; Murray and Kaitell, 2022; Newell, 1986). Interaction between these becomes a dynamic and living pedagogical component.

Maintaining a diversity awareness ensures we integrate this into our pedagogical planning and teaching. Diversity, when acknowledged and then deployed as a constraint validates the individual(s), the environment and indeed the curricular learning experience (task) as influential factors. As such, diversity transcends all components of pedagogical practice through intent, implementation and indeed impact as a uniting collective constraint. Forethought and monitoring of how we keep our diversity constraint functionally student-centred demands a meta-awareness across the planned and emergent learning. Our pre-planned pedagogy is reflexive to the emergence of potentially anticipated or unanticipated factors.

'Socially just' thinking towards 'socially just' practice

Poth uses cultural care to approach and unpack the opportunity for enquiry (2021). Such ethical reasoning necessitates that we know and understand our participating stakeholders, such as our pupils, and that we possess the acknowledged, the wherewithal and motivation to try to create equitable and accessible challenges from their standpoints rather than our own. What if we could empower our pupils as living stakeholders of the choices as they work toward the learning objectives? Structured autonomy is one means to support and facilitate such a process. In learning, providing children with authentic partial input to the 'what' and the 'how' of the learning enhances motivation and subsequent engagement (Flowerday and Schraw, 2003).

Our CCF (DfE, 2019) illuminates what we do as we plan (intent), teach (implement) and proactively reflect upon our progress (impact). With the use of a simple structured choice strategy, we invite colleagues to create a pupil stakeholder place across what has been depicted as a complex recursive process (Carse et al., 2018). This process is as it suggests. It opens the conversation to actively offer pupils choice from a series of informed options that the school and educator consider as attainable and appropriate. Pupils then come to appreciate and acquire the wherewithal to consider, discuss and agree upon the options presented. This strategy has been found to increase pupil autonomy, which as acknowledged through the CCF, is a crucial component for pupil progress (Murray and Napper-Owen, 2021). Structured choice develops an array of positive outcomes, as facilitated by intrinsic motivation.

Case study

Practically, the primary education pathway has six years of opportunity to create and implement a diversity informed and informing curricular experience across the general areas of educational athletics, dance, games, gymnastics, outdoor adventure activities and swimming. The school needs to ensure that class identity puzzles have the opportunity to grow and flourish, responding to the emerging ideas and aspirations of pupils within the wider school community mosaic.

BOLSTERING AND AFFIRMING CLASS IDENTITY THROUGH EDUCATIONAL DANCE: DANCE THROUGH CLASS IDENTITY PUZZLES

Through progression of a scope and sequence through dance, greater awareness and understanding of class members can be developed through this collaborative cultural enactment of dance. By opening the provision of dance type and style, and then facilitating pupil structured choice therein, pupils are now empowered to identify with a selection that is culturally meaningful for them. Individual pupils are asked to share a dance as enjoyed through their family and/or wider community. Pupil research is to find out the name of the dance and how it is performed. The teacher then collates these through a visual, for example, a PowerPoint, to formally validate pupil contributions. The dances are grouped into categories (as determined by what they bring in, such as formal, informal, national, celebratory). The scheme of work might then draw from each of the class emergent categories, with pupils voting on their choice per category. Pupil puzzles have been instrumental to this process, and the collective class identity further strengthened as a result of being a living part of this scope and sequence.

REFLECTION

Can you think about how you might expand these ideas across different games that are played in different places?

As teachers and pupils become more familiar with these diversity-informed practices, the entire process becomes more autonomous, which is what our CCF processes strive to attain. This cycle needs to be integrated across the primary curriculum spiral so that collective and individual understanding is progressed. This process remains interactive as to explicate, to explore, to practise and refine our diversity collective consciousness in meaningful ways for all class members. Table 10.1 provides a four-step process to illuminate and celebrate class identity as an explicit factor across our planning and teaching.

Table 10.1   Embodying recursive contextual cultural consideration through structured choice

Step 1: Be guided by our PE National Curriculum.	For primary PE, this is our Key stage 1-2 programme of study (DfE, 2013) National Curriculum for PE.	Context PE, Educational Dance as progressed through curricular fundamental movement Skills: weight transfer, balance, turning, twisting
		Explore and progress using rhythm (body, instruments, music) through movement concepts-unison, canon, solo, pairs and group. Progress into formal dances which rely on these skills. Children are competent in the skills and ready to experience a wide variety of rhythmic challenges and dances.

Step 2: Draw from pupil identity puzzle to widen scope of choices for a more culturally relevant school curriculum	What interests do each and all of my pupils have around movement, play, recreation, games, sports and activities? What aspects of their culture can they share through PE? What family-centred extracurricular activities can our school facilitate to learn a little more of the diverse interests across our attending communities? What community opportunities can I engage in to support my understanding seeking?	Consideration The teacher performs an audit of dance activities and clubs as a starting point and begins to formulate a list of choices. The wider community offers classes across jazz, hip-hop and zumba. Referring to her own identity puzzle and lived experience, the teacher suggests jazzercise.
Step 3: Facilitate structured choice	Where and how will I facilitate structured choice into the living curriculum so that I model this awareness?	Structured choice Teacher shares the list to which the pupils add as it reflects their interests. Amira suggests Bollywood and hip hop dancing. The class agrees upon what to include and what to omit, based upon their collective interests and decision.
Step 4: Revisit as the curriculum is lived across the academic year Enact structured choice and develop autonomy across all six areas of the national curriculum, ready for the next area, moving towards next year's progression	Where and how will model and facilitate structured autonomy so that pupils and other stakeholders (such as other colleagues and parents and guardians) know that I value this process and I am prepared to make this a known constraint for my practice?	Recursive In the next iteration, other pupils get to contribute as the spiral of self with class identity grows. Stephen suggests ultimate frisbee for educational games for the next class structured choice opportunity across the curricular spiral progression.

These four steps enable us to take on holistic diversity in a functional way reflective of our class membership. As we revisit and refine our processes, in response to emerging pupil needs and interests, our collective competence, availability and preparedness to do this improves.

REFLECTION

How might this approach be enacted through your current PE curricular experiences. Are there meaningful ways to extend self and class identity from the embodied PE experiences. Every child loves to move, especially when we facilitate their constraints and reflect the learning through cultural consideration. Who might you embody and create your class narrative through PE?

Joie de vivre

Play is its own construct, part of community, an extra-curricular and curricular way of being. In essence, it can be as fair and equitable as inclusive physical activity and curricular PE. Socially just PE, whereby all pupils feel and are safe and given a place and voice (Lynch et al., 2020), complements and extends these notions. All pupils should embody a positive sense of self across the spectrum of planned to unanticipated emergent opportunities as to fortify their positive self-regard. PE provides such a wonderful series of complex and exciting layers to progress across a multitude of lived learning domains (Bailey et al., 2009; Murray et al., 2018). Pedagogically, these have been integrated across a myriad of wonderfully creative and effective PE pedagogies, all of which are companionable to complementary approaches and or adaptable to bespoke school–class–educator–pupil context. You may even be creating and crafting your own pedagogy to meet aspirational curricular expectations in ways your pupils find inspiring and relevant to their lives. Current practice ought to be attuned to diversity as to assist pupils build character integrating such values as 'fairness and respect' (DfE, 2013: 1). Becoming and staying diversity aware is to proactively orient and lead through a progressive mindset (Bucher, 2015). Staying proactive through diversity thinking also a constructive part of our pedagogical practice and a means to consciously include all and avoid marginalisation of any child (Hamilton, 2021).

How do we equitably embrace internal and external diversity factors and appreciate the role of identity, through our pedagogy? This is the embodiment of our way forward, and likely, the many successful strategies you are using do just that. A systematic approach to the intent of your lessons we think might help us reduce or eliminate any unconscious bias. Through cultural consciousness and a socially just approach we can develop and improve in the same way we develop our fundamental PE skills.

The aims, the subject, the pupils, the environment; it all feels collectively complex. This we uphold as an opportunity to explore the nuances of a living curriculum through our pedagogy to reflect the complexity of self and collective identities.

CHAPTER SUMMARY

The strategy of structured choice remains a convenient and accessible means to contemplate diversity as educators offer a selection of educational activity choices aimed to meet, if not surpass, curricular outcomes. In return, pupils are provided an opportunity to empower the identity and role of the pupil in their educational progression. Indeed, it is but one example to show that we are making an explicit effort to explore, enact and embody diversity through a socially just approach by putting students in the driver's seat in the decision-making process. Culturally, we physically move with an effort which reflects, in part, who we are, what we do and how we engage with the world. Pedagogically, the educator can plan for increased use of the lived realities of pupils to make for more meaningful PE. In that way, a social identity of and through PE is created with pupils as the co-constructors and contributors to the collective experience.

References

Bailey, R., Armour, K., Kirk, D., Jess, M., Pickup, I., Sandford, R. and BERA Physical Education and Sport Pedagogy Special Interest Group (2009) The educational benefits claimed for physical education and school sport: an academic review. *Research Papers in Education*, 24(1): 1–27. **https://doi.org/10.1080/02671520701809817**

British Council (2022) *Equality Policy. Diversity Unit.* Available at: **https://www.britishcouncil.org/sites/default/files/equality_policy_2022.pdf**.

Bucher, RD. (2015) *Diversity Consciousness Opening Our Minds to People, Cultures, and Opportunities.* Upper Saddle River, NJ: Prentice Hall.

Carse, N., Jess, M. and Keay, J. (2018) Primary physical education: Shifting perspectives to move forwards. *European Physical Education Review*, 24(4): 487–502. **https://doi.org/10.1177/1356336X16688598**

Chow, J.-Y., Renshaw, I., Button, C., Davids, K. and Tan Wee Keat, C. (2012) Effective learning design for the individual: a nonlinear pedagogical approach in physical education. In A. Ovens, T. Hopper and J. Butler (eds), *Complexity Thinking in Physical Education. Reframing Curriculum, Pedagogy and Research.* London: Routledge.

DfE (2013) *National Curriculum in England: PE Programmes of Study. The Statutory Programmes of Study and Attainment Targets for Physical Education (PE) at Key Stages 1-4.* Available at: **https://www.gov.uk/government/publications/national-curriculum-in-england-physical-education-programmes-of-study**

DfE (2019) *Initial Teacher Training (ITT): Core Content Framework.* Available at: **https://www.gov.uk/government/publications/initial-teacher-training-itt-core-content-framework**

DfE (2021) *Early Years Foundation Stage (EYFS) Statutory Framework. The Standards that School and Childcare Providers Must Meet for the Learning, Development and Care of Children From Birth to 5.* Available at: **https://www.gov.uk/government/publications/early-years-foundation-stage-framework–2**

Flowerday, T. and Schraw, G. (2003) The effect of choice on cognitive and affective engagement. *Journal of Educational Research*, 96(4): 207–215.

Gabbard, C. (2021) *Lifelong Motor Development.* Lippincott Williams & Wilkins.

Giddens, A. (1991) *Modern and Self-Identity: Self and Society in the Late Modern Age.* Stanford, CA: Stanford University Press.

Graham, G., Holt/Hale, S.A., Parker, M., Hall, T. and Patton, K. (2020) *Children Moving. A Reflective Approach to Teaching Physical Education.* New York, NY: McGraw Hill.

Hamilton, P. (2021) *Diversity and Marginalisation in Childhood. A Guide for Inclusive Thinking 0–11.* London: SAGE Publications.

Korostelina, K.V. (2007) Social identity as social phenomenon and scientific concept. In *Social Identity and Conflict.* New York, NY: Palgrave Macmillan. **https://doi.org/10.1057/9780230605671_2**

Lynch, S., Sutherland, S. and Walton-Fisette, J. (2020) The A–Z of social justice physical education: part 1. *Journal of Physical Education, Recreation & Dance, 91*(4): 8–13. **https://doi.org/ 10.1080/07303084.2020.1724500**

Murray, A., Adams, S., Kaitell, E., Shaughnessy, J. and Murray, P. (2018) Using learning domains to complement primary physical education teacher education in primary school settings. *Physical Education Matters, Official Journal of the Association for Physical Education, 13*(2): 54–57.

Murray, A.M. and Napper-Owen, G. (2021) Metacognition, the METAPE-3, a New Instructional Model for Physical Education. In: Peters M.A. (eds) Encyclopedia of Teacher Education. Springer, Singapore. **https://doi.org/10.1007/978-981-13-1179-6_421-1**

Murray, A. and Kaitell, E. (2022) Educational gymnastics. Embodiment of a constraint's agility approach. In G. Griggs and V. Randall (eds), *An Introduction to Primary Physical Education*, 2nd edition. London and New York, NY: Routledge Taylor & Francis Group.

Newell, K.M. (1986) Constraints on the development of coordination. In M.G. Wade and H.T.A. Whiting (eds), *Motor Development in Children: Aspects of Coordination and Control*. Dordrecht: Martinus Nijhoff, pp. 341–360. **http://dx.doi.org/10.1007/978-94-009-4460-2_19**

Office for National Statistics (2019) *Research Report on Population Estimates by Ethnic Group and Religion*. Cultural Identity. Available at: **https://www.ons.gov.uk/peoplepopulationandcommunity/culturalidentity**

Ovens, A., Hopper, T. and Butler, J. (2008) *Complexity Thinking in Physical Education. Reframing Curriculum, Pedagogy and Research*. New York, NY: Routledge.

Poth, N.C. (2021) *Little Quick Fix: Research Ethics*. SAGE Publications Ltd.

Ryan, M., Rowan, L., Lunn Brownlee, J., Bourke, T., L'Estrange, L., Walker, S. and Churchward, P. (2020) Teacher education and teaching for diversity: a call to action. *Teaching Education*. **http://dx.doi.org/10.1080/10476210.2020.1844178**

Thorjussen, I.M. and Sisjord, M.K. (2018) Students' physical education experiences in a multi-ethnic class. *Sport, Education and Society, 23*(7): 694–706. http://dx.doi.org/10.1080/13573322. 2018.1467399

Unicef (1989) *Convention on the Rights of the Child*. Available at: **https://www.unicef.org/child-rights-convention**

11

CELEBRATING CULTURAL DIVERSITY THROUGH ARTS IN THE PRIMARY SCHOOL

SUSAN OGIER

KEYWORDS: ARTS; CONTEMPORARY; CULTURE; DIVERSITY; ENGAGEMENT; IDENTITY; INTERPRETATION

CHAPTER OBJECTIVES

The aims of this chapter are:

- To consider the context for exploring arts and culture with primary children within the current educational climate.
- To address the urgency of helping children to understand one another, and members of a wider society, through a deepening sense of their own cultural heritage, as well as exposure to those of others.
- To explore the relevance of collaborative research projects, such as European Union (EU) funded *Images and Identity* (2010) and *Creative Connections* (2014).
- To suggest that by engaging children with (and in) artistic experiences that celebrate a wide range of world cultures, teachers can reduce the formation of stereotypical views, and promote tolerance and respect for others, embracing difference.

CCF ITE links

1.5	1.5 A culture of mutual trust and respect supports effective relationships.
1.6	High-quality teaching has a long-term positive effect on pupils' life chances, particularly for children from disadvantaged backgrounds.
4.7	High-quality classroom talk can support pupils to articulate key ideas, consolidate understanding and extend their vocabulary.
5.2	Seeking to understand pupils' differences, including their different levels of prior knowledge and potential barriers to learning, is an essential part of teaching.

Artists often explore the characteristics that determine our personal and social identity. They construct a sense of who we are as individuals, as a society, or as a nation. They question stereotypes and conventions while exploring attributes such as gender, sexuality, race, nationality, and heritage.

Tate essay: *Cultural Identity* (Available at: **https://www.tate.org.uk/artist-rooms/collection/themes/cultural-identity**)

Introduction

In this chapter, we shall take a look at the role of arts education as a means to broaden children's outlook on the world and its people. The arts have held a central place in communities since the beginning of humanity and are present in many forms in every single culture across the world. The universality of modes of expression afforded by arts engagement, whether through dance, music, visual art or many of the other artforms, creates a range of alternative means by which we can learn about the past, understand the present and contemplate the future. It allows us to communicate freely across cultures without geographical or verbal language barriers. The intention of this chapter is to explore ways that we can embrace the arts as a means of drawing on – and expanding – children's cultural capital in any primary classroom.

The value of learning in the arts

The value of engaging primary-aged children in arts education is well documented in terms of their holistic development (Ogier, 2019). Ogier and Tutchell (2021) argue that the arts act as an agent for change, a vehicle for depth of learning, provide pathways for social engagement and act as an entry point for many children to become curious and critical thinkers. They describe five 'Cs' – five critical skills that can be facilitated by immersing children in arts education, and all of these combined are key components for developing children as responsible and respectful global citizens:

1. **Creativity**: *having the ability to think imaginatively, express oneself and to develop fresh ideas are essential to innovation and progress.*

2. **Collaboration**: *Working together for a common purpose teaches children that their contribution is important, which is perfect for the nature of collaborative practice in arts projects.*

3. **Confidence**: *The arts create a safe space for children to explore their talents and build their confidence, and so they are more likely to take risks and step out of their comfort zone to try new things in other areas of their lives.*

4. **Cultural Awareness and Empathy**: *The arts provide a unique platform to discuss many different cultures, socioeconomic levels and current events that affect our lives.*

5. **Critical Thinking**: *The arts necessitate a creative process which includes conceptual and interpretational thinking that helps build critical thinking skills including observation, reasoning and problem-solving.*

(Ogier and Tutchell, 2021: 10)

These five Cs are all vital for child development, but for the purposes of this chapter, the salient one, perhaps, is point 4: that the arts provide a platform for exploring cultural differences: understanding one another and accepting different ways of 'being'. In addition, the arts also help children understand themselves as individuals, and therefore I might argue that this is where we need to start.

The self and others: the notion of multiple identities

Michael Rosen once asked, 'what good is an education in which children do not learn about themselves?' (BBC, 2010), and certainly this is true of our job in teaching young children at primary level. This is often the place where children first learn to rub along with others outside of their immediate family or social sect. It is at primary school and in Early Years settings that children discover alternative ways of living and being and find out that not everyone has the same life experiences as they do. As children become more exposed to a wide variety of learning experiences, personalities, points of views and environments in which they can develop a sense of social identification, they are adding new dimensions to their own thoughts, skill sets and understanding of their world. A child's sense of personal identity is without doubt a root from which they will grow, by understanding who they are, where they are from, what they like or dislike, who their friends are, what activities they enjoy, what they wear for what different occasions and the list can go on.

The exploration of multiple identities can help children to develop empathy and socialisation skills. A study by Gaither et al. (2019) showed that meta-awareness of all these dimensions can be useful in terms of developing children's creative and flexible thinking. Through research using three separate experiments, the team worked with children aged between six and seven years old, specifically because it was deemed that they would already have developed a sense of knowing themselves, and they, at this age, would be able to deal with complexity of situations in a more thoughtful way. The highlights of the research showed that:

- Prompting children to think about their own multiple identities, versus various control conditions, boosted their creativity and their ability to think flexibly about social categories, such as race.

- The findings highlighted positive consequences of acknowledging one's own identities as a pathway that could promote more positive intergroup relations as children develop.

In an already packed curriculum, we might reflect on just where the space is to explore and celebrate children's developing understanding of themselves as multifaceted, complex, socially driven beings: learning in and through the arts can provide that arena. The following case study will show how this might work in practice.

Case study: images and identity

Art education is concerned with self-expression and exploring personal identification. Art teachers routinely encourage their students to value art-making as a psychological manifestation of their social, cultural and individual identities, and to use visual images as a means to exchange and communicate their feelings and ideas.

(Mason, 2019)

As Mason describes in the above quote, art practice is a socially constructed arena where themes, concerns, issues and emotions can be explored in a safe space. This is what artists do: they offer a reflection of the society in which they exist, so that we, the audience, can begin to question ourselves, our actions and thoughts, and to see our humanity more clearly. *Images and Identity* was an EU-funded, Comenius action research project that ran from 2010 to 2014 and was underpinned by this notion. It was devised to examine how digital art and citizenship education could facilitate an exploration of children's notions of European identity, starting with the self and children's personal stories. Universities in six countries participated in the research: Czech Republic, England, Ireland, Germany, Malta and Portugal, each working with different school age groups, including primary-aged children. At the time of this project, the United Kingdom was still within the EU, and in the curriculum citizenship education, as well as time for arts subjects were showing decline in English schools, as the focus was becoming more intent on the 'core' subject areas of Mathematics and English (DfE, 2015). For this project, the English team researchers worked with four Year five classes in multi-ethnic, London-based primary schools, where many of the children spoke English as an additional language and had family backgrounds from all around the world. The projects were designed to maximise both artistic creativity and rich dialogue between children and the teachers involved, so the children worked collaboratively to develop a sense of community (Lave and Wenger, 1998) within an open-ended brief. The underpinning research concept was to investigate how far children's stereotypical views of themselves and the 'other' affected their personal identification, and whether this could be expanded to encompass more empathy towards differences, and more understanding of similarities.

Zander (2004) discusses the value of the art classroom in that more scope is available for children to express and voice their ideas and opinions openly. She says that it can become an emotionally safe space in which discussion can take place not only during art-making but also through engaging with a wide range of existing artworks from a variety of cultural and historical contexts. By using strategies such as mind-mapping and developing a community of practice, the children involved in the projects developed a deep understanding of both personal and shared cultural identity. Complex concepts such as society, democracy, technology, communication, symbol, politics, community and traditions were explored and discussed, and children have vastly moved on their initial stereotypical notions of 'food', 'clothes', 'friends', 'pets', etc. (See Further Reading for two articles related to this case study.)

Case study: creative connections

Creative Connections built upon the success of the Images and Identity project by securing further Comenius funding (2012–2014) with some of the same partners involved, including Czech Republic, Portugal, England, Ireland and with the addition of Finland and Spain (Catalan). Twenty four schools across those countries took part in the work. The project focused on developing the 'child's voice' by facilitating artwork to be created, discussed and shared over a digital platform using online translation facilities. The (then) new technology gave children the opportunity to communicate without language barriers and learn about each other's lives, thereby improving cultural understanding through the medium of art. The children's responses to one another were of support and friendship, acceptance and interest in the diversity of cultures that they encountered.

You can have a look at the website, with free resources and lesson plans available, and browse the Connected Gallery, which houses artworks that were used to inspire the children's conversations and creations on this link: **http://www.ese.ipvc.pt/dc/EN/AA00.html**.

What do we mean by cultural diversity in arts education?

UNESCO's *Convention on the Protection and Promotion of the Diversity of Cultural Expressions* (2005) gives us a useful definition:

> *'Cultural diversity' refers to the manifold ways in which the cultures of groups and societies find expression. These expressions are passed on within and among groups and societies. Cultural diversity is made manifest not only through the varied ways in which the cultural heritage of humanity is expressed, augmented and transmitted through the variety of cultural expressions, but also through diverse modes of artistic creation, production, dissemination, distribution and enjoyment, whatever the means and technologies used.*

(2005: 7)

The notion of *expression* is important. This means that the languages afforded by various artforms are recognised as holding a degree of status that allows the transmission of ideas to create a common understanding in ways that are not afforded by other means, such as written text or verbal communication. Basic human values are part of this picture, and this is why the arts are so well placed as a platform for building common understanding across disparate groups. In fact, the agreement goes on to give a list of what this means as terms of reference in forming a common understanding for the signatories of the agreement. The long list cites a wide range of key points, but the first five (as we seem to be dealing in 5s in this chapter!) are as follows:

- *Affirming* that cultural diversity is a defining characteristic of humanity,

- *Conscious* that cultural diversity forms a common heritage of humanity and should be cherished and preserved for the benefit of all,

- *Being aware* that cultural diversity creates a rich and varied world, which increases the range of choices and nurtures human capacities and values, and therefore is a mainspring for sustainable development for communities, peoples and nations,

- **Recalling** that cultural diversity, flourishing within a framework of democracy, tolerance, social justice and mutual respect between peoples and cultures, is indispensable for peace and security at the local, national and international levels,

- **Celebrating** the importance of cultural diversity for the full realisation of human rights and fundamental freedoms proclaimed in the Universal Declaration of Human Rights and other universally recognised instruments.

(UNESCO, 2005: 3)

REFLECTION

What do you understand of the term *cultural diversity* and how this relates to *engagement in the arts*?

How do you think the five key points applies to your work with children and their education in primary schools?

We can see from these definitions that arts and culture play a huge role in how we articulate the fundamental value of cultural diversity in our own society and across the world. Why on earth wouldn't we start this conversation with children in our schools at a young age? This would certainly help build a more compassionate and creative future through using the arts as a vehicle for understanding one another. As we now have a climate crisis to contend with, we need to be open and responsive to our fellow world citizens and come together in securing a safe world for the future – creativity plays an enormous part in the crucial success of this, as explained by Mar and Ang (2015):

> *Cultural diversity is now seen as an essential requirement of sustainable development, because a world where diversity flourishes increases the range of choices for people and communities, thus nurturing their capacities for creativity and innovation. Moreover, promoting and protecting diversity is essential for world peace, as it boosts the potential for creative dialogues resulting from interactions of diverse cultures, both nationally and globally.*

(2015: 5)

Recently within schools the term *cultural capital* has become more prevalent. There are, however, issues in interpreting what is meant by this phrase and how this could be used to suggest a cannon of 'accepted' works. The question that we should be considering is whose cultural capital should we be considering? Ofsted's Education Inspection Framework specifically addresses the idea of cultural capital as a focus during inspection:

> *As part of making the judgement about quality of education, inspectors will consider the extent to which schools are equipping pupils with the knowledge and cultural capital they need to succeed in life. Ofsted's understanding of this knowledge and cultural capital matches the understanding set out in the aims of the national curriculum. It is the essential knowledge that pupils need to be educated citizens, introducing them to the best that has been thought and said, and helping to engender an appreciation of human creativity and achievement.*

(2021: 10)

What does it mean therefore to be 'educated citizens' and how has this come to focus on Western Art? In accepting a view of 'cultural capital' with a specific if unacknowledged focus on Western Art, we negate or ignore the cultural achievements of others.

What has global citizenship got to do with learning in the arts?

The way that all of our lives are affected by globalisation is highly apparent. The old saying 'what a small world!' has never been more true. Pressing global issues, such as climate change, have perhaps, as never before, focused our attention on just exactly how small we are as a planet, and there are many reports, such as the Dasgupta Report (2021), that call for collaboration by every nation to save nature – and ourselves. The Dasgupta Report highlights the key role that each and every one of us, as individuals, has to play in how we attempt to save life in all its forms, and in this way we all have responsibilities that go hand in hand with our rights as citizens. Sustainability, if nothing else, is a key driver for educating children to become active participants in global advancement, and there is no doubt that children will need the skills highlighted by the five 'Cs' earlier in this chapter. Once again, the arts are a good place to explore difficult, even frightening, issues with young children as they are able to find their voice and make clear their communication through the many modes of expression that should be available to them: though art, dance, music, song, poetry, designing, drama, photography, film – the list goes on. Can you remember the advent of the pandemic? Travelling was impossible, and physical connection with our loved ones evaporated, but through creativity and digital technology the way we communicated with our friends and family changed almost overnight. Children and young people have the world at their fingertips through digital devices. How different is this from even one generation ago? Children growing up today ARE global citizens, and it is important that they know just what that means and what their responsibilities as such are.

Decolonising the arts curriculum

In today's world, we are extremely conscious that there is a need to decolonise the curriculum and to move away from tokenistic references to 'multiculturism' in the classroom. In the arts, this is not a difficult leap to make, as there are many wonderful examples of Black and ethnic artists whose work can inspire and enrich children's lives. By viewing their work and knowing their stories, we can begin to understand one another at a deeper level and help young people feel empowered to do the same.

For many years in the 1980s and 1990s, schools sought to address aspects of different cultures and life experiences, and this was commonly known as *multicultural education*. This was a bid to acknowledge or study a different view or a different way of living and being, by observing different cultures from one's own (Cahan and Kocur, 2011). There were books on it and courses on it, and lesson plans are still found online today, via a quick search – *'The topic this term is "Africa", so in art – let's look at African masks and make one'*. However, the term *multiculturalism* has taken on a slightly different meaning than the one that was advocated all those years ago, which is maybe why we don't hear the term so often now. Cahan and Kocur state that:

Generally missing from multicultural education is an approach that connects everyday experience, social critique and creative expression. When the focus is shifted to issues and ideas that students truly care about and are relevant within a larger life world context, art becomes a vital means of reflecting on the nature of society and social existence.

(2011: 7)

So, the word *multi* (meaning many) added to *culture* is self-explanatory when broken down in this way, and we can see why the tokenistic approach has failed. Our 'cultural capital' is now one that brings together the many *cultures* that we are exposed to, through travelling, browsing the internet, food, music, podcasts, going to galleries and museums, theatre, watching TV, through our friends and families – and all the other ways that we learn about the diversity of our world. The arts are essential as a tool that helps us develop an understanding of the values and traditions across societies that are not our own, but we then naturally incorporate some of those into our lives – and make them our own (Figure 11.1).

REFLECTION

Listen to the podcast 'How arts and culture can help decolonise the curriculum' to help you to consider the role the arts in addressing issues of race and curriculum: **https://www.tes.com/ news/how-arts-and-culture-can-help-decolonise-curriculum**.

Exploring cultural diversity through contemporary art

There is surely no better way to introduce children to understanding cultures that are different from their own than by engaging them with artworks by contemporary artists from around the world and at

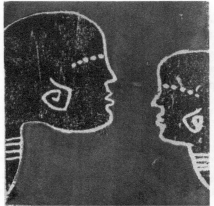

Figure 11.1   Exploring the concept of the 'other' in relation to culture through printmaking

home. The use of contemporary artworks in the primary classroom has been a rather slow train arriving, with many art schemes continuing to advocate 'safe' contextual references from art history. There are reasons for this, such as availability of appropriate resources and space, a lack of confidence in interpreting what might be seen as art that is difficult to read (for example, Conceptual Art), or that there are pedagogical 'risks' that throw up a range of dilemmas for the primary teacher (Adams, 2010; Charman and Ross, 2004). Over the past decade or so, we have certainly become risk-adverse in our profession, and the narrow and prescriptive curriculum within which we work has encouraged this. If we can move away from repeatedly using white, Western, deceased male artists such as Van Gogh and Warhol (as wonderful as they are) and towards a more diverse range of living and breathing artists from a broader spectrum of backgrounds, we will increase and develop that important cultural capital for every child. Contemporary art reflects the society in which we exist, opening up questions that can be difficult to answer, while at the same time encouraging us to think critically about those challenging issues. In art we can afford to take a different path, due to the very nature of the subject area, and open that door marked 'Uncertainty' and embrace it.

Case study: Chloe

Chloe, an art specialist early career teacher, wanted to expand the range of artists that were being studied across the West London primary school in which she worked. This was to better reflect the diversity of the children and families attending the school and to update the existing scheme of work for art, which had been in use for many years without review.

In collaboration with the class teachers, she planned to hold a 'round the world in eight artists' exhibition, so that teachers were motivated to complete the art projects with the class by a certain date. Each year group chose a different area of the world and researched contemporary artists to show the children and to inspire their own artwork. Reception class loved exploring the patterns and dots of Japanese artist Yayoi Kusama from Japan; Year 2 used Guyana-born Frank Bowling's colourful, textured painting to develop their own experiments in paint; Year 4 used Brazilian artist, Vik Muniz work on 'surfaces' to investigate texture and shape through collage; Year 6 looked at Ai Wei Wei to create their own text-based work in ceramics.

REFLECTION

How confident do you feel to use contemporary artworks that reflect our diverse society?

Have a look at some of these artists' work online and build a bank of resources to run your project to explore our diverse world based on contemporary art.

Consider where and how you can celebrate cultural diversity through the arts in your primary curriculum.

CHAPTER SUMMARY

In this chapter, we have considered current issues in the primary classroom and how we might develop a deeper understanding of the 'other' in an effort to promote empathy and tolerance through the arts and creativity. We have explored the notion of multiple identities by drawing on case studies and contextualised these to develop the argument that children of primary school age are essentially engaged in finding out about themselves within a wider community. We have reflected on the importance of UNESCO's *Convention on the Protection and Promotion of the Diversity of Cultural Expressions* (2005) to validate the role that the arts play in developing a sense of our humanity and connection to others who share our world. We have looked at ways we might use the wonderful gift that we have in the arts to promote a decolonised curriculum and suggested ways that you can begin to make changes in your own practice, to build a common cultural capital with the children in your class.

Further reading

Collins, F. and Ogier, S. (2012) Expressing identity: the role of dialogue in teaching citizenship through art. *Education 3–13, International Journal of Primary, Elementary and Early Years Education, 41*(6): 617–632.

Crossick, G. and Kaszynska, P. (2016) *Understanding the Value of Arts and Culture.* Available at: **https://ahrc.ukri.org/documents/publications/cultural-value-project-final-report/**

Healy, M. and Richardson, M. (2017) Images and identity: children constructing a sense of belonging to Europe. *European Research Journal, 6*(4): 440–454. Available at: **https://journals. sagepub.com/doi/full/10.1177/1474904116674015**

References

Adams, J. (2010) Risky choices: the dilemmas of introducing contemporary art practices into schools. *British Journal of Sociology of Education, 31*(6): 683–701.

Cahan, S. and Kocur, Z. (2011) Contemporary art and multicultural education. In E. Joo, J. Keehn and J. Ham-Robert (eds), *Rethinking Contemporary Art and Multicultural Education.* New Museum, London, New York, NY: Routledge, pp. 3–16.

Charman, H. and Ross, M. (2004) *Contemporary Art and the Role of Interpretation, Tate Papers No 2, Autumn 2004, Tate.* Available at: **https://www.tate.org.uk/research/publications/tate-papers/02/contemporary-art-and-the-role-of-interpretation**

Dasgupta, P. (2021) *The Economics of Biodiversity: The Dasgupta Review.* London: HM Treasury. Available at: **https://assets.publishing.service.gov.uk/government/uploads/system/uploads/attachment_data/file/962785/The_Economics_of_Biodiversity_The_Dasgupta_Review_Full_Report.pdf**

DfE (2015) *Programme of Study, Citizenship, KS1 and 2.* Online. Available at: **https://assets.publishing.service.gov.uk/government/uploads/system/uploads/attachment_data/file/402173/Programme_of_Study_KS1_and_2.pdf**

Gaither, S.E., Fan, S. and Kinzler, K. (2019) Thinking about multiple identities boosts children's flexible thinking. *Developmental Science, 23*(1). Online. Available at: **https://doi.org/10.1111/desc.12871**.

Lave, J. and Wenger, E. (1998) *Communities of Practice, Learning, Meaning and Identity.* Cambridge: Cambridge University Press.

Mar, P. and Ang, I. (2015) *Promoting Diversity of Cultural Expressions in Arts in Australia.* Sydney, NSW: Australia Council for the Arts. Available at: **https://www.westernsydney.edu.au/__data/assets/pdf_file/0004/978817/diversity_of_cultural_expression_report.pdf**

Mason, R. (2019) Creating a space for exploring self-identity. In S. Ogier (ed.), *The Broad and Balanced Curriculum in Primary Schools: Educating the Whole Child.* London: SAGE, Learning Matters.

Ofsted (2021) Education Inspection Framework. **https://www.gov.uk/government/publications/education-inspection-framework/education-inspection-framework**

Ogier, S. (2019) *The Broad and Balanced Curriculum in Primary Schools: Educating the Whole Child.* London: SAGE, Learning Matters.

Ogier, S. and Tutchell, S. (2021) *Teaching Arts in the Primary School.* London: SAGE, Learning Matters.

Rosen, M. (2010) *Imagine: Art is Child's Play.* BBC iplayer (no longer available)

UNESCO's Convention on the Protection and Promotion of the Diversity of Cultural Expressions (2005) Paris, France. Online: Available at: **https://en.unesco.org/creativity/sites/creativity/files/convention2005_basictext_en.pdf#page=15**

Zander, M.J. (2004) Becoming dialogic: creating a place for dialogue in the art classroom. *Art Education, 57*(3): 48–53.

12

CONNECTING WITH THE NATURAL WORLD THROUGH ANIMATED FILMS FOR CHILDREN: A POSTHUMAN PERSPECTIVE

KERENZA GHOSH

KEYWORDS: ANIMATED FILM; ARTS-BASED RESPONSES; ENVIRONMENT; NATURAL WORLD; POSTHUMANISM; THE SEA

CHAPTER OBJECTIVES

The aims of this chapter are:

- Reflect on diversity in terms of our connection as humans with the natural world.
- Consider opportunities to introduce posthumanist philosophies into the classroom.
- Develop teaching approaches that enable children to explore animated film.

CCF ITE links

1.1	Teachers have the ability to affect and improve the well-being, motivation and behaviour of all pupils.
1.2	Teachers are key role models who can influence the attitudes, values and behaviours of their pupils.
2.1	Learning involves a lasting change in pupils' capabilities and understanding.
3.7	In all subject areas, pupils learn new ideas by linking those ideas to existing knowledge, organising the knowledge into increasingly complex mental models (or schemata) carefully sequencing teaching to facilitate this process is important.

If we care about our common future and the common future of our descendants, we should all in part be naturalists.

(Dasgupta, 2021: 6)

Diversity and the natural world

Inviting children to reflect upon their relationship with the natural world may seem like an unusual approach to the topic of diversity. But when we consider life on our planet and its various ecosystems – its biodiversity – opportunities to broaden our notion of what constitutes diversity become apparent. Understanding our place as humans within the (bio)diversity of our planet involves adopting a posthuman perspective. Posthuman theory focuses on the interdependence between humans, animals and the environment, subjects with which children will be familiar through stories, culture and everyday experiences. Nurturing children's connection with the natural world can occur in assorted ways, from real-life encounters in environments such as local parks, woodlands and coastal landscapes, to depictions of nature in folklore, fantasy and film. Accordingly, this chapter presents a study of animated films *Song of the Sea* (Moore, 2014) and *Ponyo on the Cliff by the Sea* (Miyazaki, 2008) – two fantasy narratives about childhood and the sea. Given the significance of animated film in children's culture, the chapter will demonstrate how these animations can provide a fruitful medium to explore posthumanist ideas with young children in the primary classroom. Related discussions can contribute to children's interest in sea life and sea creatures as well as their broader education regarding nature. Currently, 'nature studies' is not a formalised subject in England's education systems, although its inclusion in the curriculum is strongly recommended in a 2021 publication commissioned by the UK government, entitled *The Economics of Biodiversity: The Dasgupta Review*. The review concludes with the message that 'Connecting with nature needs to be woven throughout our lives' (Dasgupta, 2021: 498). This powerful statement draws attention to nature as an entity which unifies us all and of which we are all a part. The following section will provide a basic introduction to posthumanism, with insight into how related concepts may be identified in animated films for children, so that teachers may begin to think about how associated exploration could develop in the classroom.

REFLECTION

Think about your own recent interactions with nature: this can be in your local environment or further afield.

Where were you? What did you see and hear? How did you feel? What did you enjoy the most? What surprised you? In what way(s) did you feel connected with that environment? What words come to mind when you describe your interaction with nature?

Posthumanism: a brief introduction

Posthumanism is a form of philosophical enquiry into humanity and its integral connection with the rest of the world, be that animal, cybernetic or environmental. As a theoretical approach, it focuses on the interdependence between human, nature and machine. Often, posthumanism is thought of in terms of artificial intelligence (AI), including robots, machinery and cyborgs, all of which are integrated within modern human life; indeed, you can probably think of examples, both real and fictional. A number of animated films offer intriguing depictions of the relationship between humans and AI, for example *Big Hero 6* (2014), *The Mitchells vs. the Machines* (2021) and *Wall-E* (2008). Whilst these animations reflect a contemporary trend in technological development and a growing desire to understand how our lives are woven in with machines, cybernetics and AI, the interrelation of humans with the natural world is equally compelling. During the COVID-19 pandemic, nature has proven to be a source of comfort, respite, awe, wonder and learning for children and adults alike, with many personal anecdotes of newfound appreciation for time spent in outdoors environments. Conversely, our collective increasing awareness of climate change, the force of nature and the unprecedented impact of humans upon the environment means that children themselves are facing the aftermath of environmental disasters that are both manmade and natural (Malone et al., 2020). Overall, this present environmental context is cause for both celebration and concern, calling for our relationship with nature to be not only maintained but also strengthened. Opportunities to reflect with children upon our place within the natural world are therefore increasingly significant.

Posthumanist theory emerged in the late 20th century as a reaction to the anthropocentric ('human-centred') claims of humanism, which position the human at the centre of all life and as being superior to nature. In other words, anthropocentrism asserts that the human is entirely distinct from animals, environments and other nonhuman entities; is the source of meaning and history; and shares a universal essence with other human beings (Badmington, 2004). Theorist N. Katherine Hayles recognises that posthumanism can evoke 'understandably negative reactions' (1999: 283) since it suggests there could be something above, beyond, and – most provocatively – after the presence of humans. It should be noted, however, that posthumanism is not about totally discarding the human or the quality of acting humanely. Indeed, the human is both usefully decentred by posthumanist philosophy and nonetheless crucial to it, since humans are always enmeshed with the more-than-human world and ultimately are inseparable from the environment (Alaimo, 2010). If these ideas seem somewhat befuddling, do not be deterred – posthumanism is a broad concept which produces 'different and even irreconcilable definitions' (Wolfe, 2010: xi). It is on account of this ambiguity that posthumanist theory actively generates valuable opportunities for questioning our place in the natural world. The posthuman perspective I prioritise in this chapter invites us to consider the interconnectedness between humans and nature by exploring the boundaries that have typically been used to mark us as separate from other living entities. As Louise Westling explains, posthumanism 'helps to define the human place within the ecosystem by interrogating or erasing the boundary that has been assumed to set our species apart from the rest of the living community' (2006: 30). The boundaries to be erased stem from established binary opposites including human/animal, land/sea, nature/culture and reality/fantasy, all of which feature thematically in the animated films *Ponyo* and *Song of the Sea*, examined later in this chapter. Resisting these binary oppositions 'does not mean *abandoning* them' (Murris, 2016: 202), since binaries can provide children with a way to read the world and a narrative tool to engage their imagination, intellect and emotion. Rather, posthumanism involves exploring, challenging and questioning said binaries, along with interrogating the control that humans have traditionally sought to exert over the environment.

Ironically, the posthuman potential of children's fiction can succumb to reinforced anthropocentric conventions. For instance, consider how *The Little Mermaid* fairy tale by Hans Cristian Andersen might be seen to contest the binary opposites mentioned above. By escaping her ocean home, the mermaid defies the limits of underwater and earth-dwelling species, to become both of sea *and* land. Ultimately, however, she finds herself beholden to unrequited *human* love, leaving her broken-hearted and causing her death. This example shows how stories, when read from a posthuman perspective, have the potential to radically subvert the binaries that have been established by a human order of the world; at the same time, the subversive features of these same stories may reinforce systems of human control and authority. After all, as Robyn McCallum argues, children's fiction is largely 'dominated by humanist conceptions of the individual, the self and the child' (1999: 257). Yet while humanism may be standard in children's literature, the subversive aspects of these narratives nonetheless have the capacity to critique, and even radically transcend, human hierarchies and dominant cultural ideologies (Jaques, 2015). Taking a posthuman perspective enables us to uncover the emerging complexities, and often the contradictions, in stories which can be read as disrupting those ideologies that see human, animal and environment as separate. Such separation can be challenged by an approach that values diversity. With this in mind, we can start to appreciate how diversity, posthumanism and children's literature can be relevant to one another.

Diversity can be thought of as a continuum between sameness and difference, which we negotiate in trying to understand our relationship with the world around us. This negotiation of similarity and dissimilarity – namely, the essence of identity and being (known as ontology) – is at the core of all philosophy including posthumanism. Since stories produced for children are always concerned – at least implicitly – with how a subject might negotiate their relationship with others while navigating the experiences of growing up (Flanagan, 2017), diversity is thereby fundamental to children's literature. Posthuman theorist Donna Haraway explains that seeing ourselves as entwined with the existence of more than just the humans around us involves being conscious of and responsive to 'relations of significant otherness' (2003: 8). These ideas are beginning to find their place more explicitly in the primary classroom, where research has shown how picturebooks can be used to investigate posthumanist ideas with children, with key implications for pedagogy (Murris, 2015). Discussions around posthumanism have the potential to intrigue children, who typically 'are fascinated with the boundaries between humans and other animals, and between animate and inanimate' because they enjoy 'the sheer pleasure of the surprise, of seeing that there *could* be other ways to be' (Boyd, 2007: 224–225). Because stories bring together beings that are imaginary, impossible and real, any attempts to draw boundaries between reality and fantasy become challenging and, consistent with the aims of posthumanism, invite questions around our place in the natural world. Such stories can of course be told through animated film: the 'imaginative and boundary-blurring' properties (Jaques, 2015: 6) of children's literature – including animation – provides an appropriate space to explore posthuman ideas and facilitate dialogue around how those borders between human and nonhuman might become more fluid. The potential to use film as a pedagogical context for post-humanism is outlined in the next section.

Animated film and children's culture

The moving image occupies a central role in children's cultural experiences outside school (Marsh and Millard, 2000; Evans, 2004). Given the capacity of film to draw young audiences, the medium provides educators with an effective means to explore complex, nuanced stories and challenging ideas, including those associated with posthumanism. In the primary classroom, responding to film through discussion, writing, drawing and storyboarding has been found to positively impact children's creative, cultural and critical responses (Maine, 2015; Reid, 2015; Watts, 2007). Innovative approaches to film production have resulted in a variety of animation aesthetics, including CGI, hand-drawn and stop motion, providing a rich visual arena for children's engagement. Moreover, animation is compelling because of its intrinsic multimodal qualities: visual imagery; depiction of movement; and the use of audio – both through music and sound effects (Serafini, 2014). As seen in *Ponyo* and *Song of the Sea*, this multi-modality means the animation medium is well suited to conveying an abundance of creatures, eco-systems and diverse ways to be.

A brief note on feature-length films in the classroom

These feature-length films can be explored together or individually, in the classroom or a film club. Dividing the film into segments for viewing over a series of sessions will give children space to reflect on key details. Another option is to only show selected scenes as part of a teaching sequence, providing verbal plot summaries of skipped scenes: this approach will allow time for children to watch the whole film on another occasion. A DVD copy will enable scenes to be paused and rewatched with ease. Screen captures of still images from key scenes are an effective resource to engage children in close observation, discussion and annotation in pairs or small groups.

Life below water

Before thinking further about the two films, it is worth reflecting on how the sea makes our planet habitable for humankind. Rainwater, drinking water, weather, climate, coastlines, food and even the air we breathe are ultimately provided and governed by the ocean – this itself is an interesting posthuman consideration. Sadly, marine ecosystems and costal ways of life are steadily deteriorating due to pollution caused by humans. Preserving the ocean is therefore a priority for marine biodiversity and our collective futures: one United Nations Sustainable Development Goal aims to conserve the sea and to use its resources responsibly. Yet despite its significance to all life, the ocean is an abstract and mysterious place for humans: many of us, children included, have limited – if indeed any – direct experience of the sea and life below water. Animated films can therefore be an important source for children to discover the wonders of the ocean and our connection with the sea.

Diverse folklore traditions

Folklore about the sea informs both films, providing audiences with insight into Irish and Japanese culture. *Song of the Sea*, produced by Irish animation company Cartoon Saloon, draws on Celtic folktales of the selkie, mystical creatures who transform from seal into human. Film writer Tomm Moore based his story on a personal experience: holidaying in the west coast of Ireland, he and his family were devastated to see dead seals washing up on the shoreline, culled by people who blame seals for falling fish stocks. Such human aggression toward nature would never have occurred in bygone years, when there was strong belief in the supernatural and harming seals was bad luck. Consequently, Moore felt compelled to create *Song of the Sea* as a way to restore Celtic folklore traditions and our connection with nature (Maessen and Umé, 2015). Interestingly, Moore cites the films of Hayao Miyazaki as influential to his work: Miyazaki's *Ponyo* draws on Japanese folklore, namely the tale of *Urashima Taro*, about a man who saves a sea turtle (Ozaki, 1908). Japan's indigenous religion, Shintōism, sees all things – including objects, environments and animals – as being imbued with a spiritual essence. Shintō beliefs are embedded in the narrative of *Ponyo* and are, I suggest, in keeping with posthuman philosophy. Folklore and religion often present a fusion of culture and nature, addressing the inseparability and integration between human experience and understanding of the natural world. Sharing this context with children will draw their attention to cultural diversity and provide a foundation for thinking about posthuman ideas within these films.

Posthumanism in *Ponyo* and *Song of the Sea*

At this point we can identify how the animations encompass posthuman ideas, including: interconnection between children and the ocean; challenging binaries and valuing (bio)diversity. These ideas are not mutually exclusive and resulting overlap has potential to invite interesting discussion with children.

- *Interconnection between children and the ocean*: In stories, physical transformation between human and animal form symbolises an integral connection between humans and the sea. Transformation narratives seem to express 'our sense that we both are animals and are different from other animals', which as David Whitley explains, 'can be a disturbing, as well as vital, conception' (2016: 208). These animations feature main characters who are simultaneously of land and sea: Ponyo is part-goldfish, comes from the ocean, runs atop waves and walks on land, eventually becoming a human child; Saoirse lives on land as a human and swims underwater as a seal. In selkie form, Saoirse experiences freedom and joy previously absent from her life on land. Her entwined existence is bittersweet, however, since Saoirse's family are both created and torn apart by their interconnection with the ocean and its magic. Likewise, Ponyo rides the waves with playful exuberance in order to reach Sōsuke (the human boy whom she befriends); yet Ponyo's wild actions cause rising tides and a tsunami that ultimately devastates the town, displacing its residents. These moments raise questions about our connection with, and separation from, the natural world: talking with children about Ponyo's and Saoirse's relationship with the sea, and their transformative abilities, invites a posthuman perspective. Moreover, by questioning the interconnection between humans and the sea, children can begin to reconsider states of being: How is the ocean similar to, and different from, humans? What does it mean to be 'alive'? How might this effect the way in which we treat the sea and the creatures living within it? Open discussion and dialogue pave the way in addressing these philosophical questions. By acknowledging the entangled environments in which we exist, these discussions aim to develop children's critical reflections of the connection between nature and humanity.

- *Challenging binaries, including human/animal, land/sea, nature/culture, reality/fantasy*: Alongside human–animal transformations, children may enjoy exploring how these films challenge other binaries. *Song of the Sea* is set in parallel worlds – one real, one magical – mirroring one other: the quiet sea becomes an enchanted underwater world inhabited by selkies; city streets are magical underground tunnels, home to faeries; and granny's house in the city resembles the owl-witch's hut in the woods, suggesting a strong connection between the real and the mythical environments. Music weaves together folklore culture and the natural world. Through its title, *Song of the Sea* draws attention to the Irish folk melody at the film's narrative core (Coulais, 2014). When Saoirse plays this song on the conch shell left behind by her selkie mother, she discovers the magical coat that connects her to the selkie heritage. Saoirse is mute, but must find her voice and sing to break the owl-witch's spell, liberate ancient faerie folk and save her human family. Children can consider the following: What are the similarities between the real and magical worlds? How are they different? What connects these worlds? How does the song of the title create an overlap between nature and culture? With such questions children can consider how the film challenges land/sea, nature/culture and reality/fantasy binaries. Similar questions can be asked of *Ponyo*.

- *Valuing (bio)diversity*: In both films the ocean is a powerful, distinctive realm, teeming with varied life forms. The opening sequence of *Ponyo* immerses us in an underwater world inhabited by jellyfish, crabs, plankton and bioluminescent cuttlefish, among others. The authenticity of this scene is generated through the diversity of deep-sea creatures and hand-drawn animation techniques that give each creature individuality. The soundtrack to this scene, entitled 'Deep Sea Pastures' (Hisaishi, 2008), evokes the ebb and flow of water and may in turn be described as mysterious, gentle, magical, humorous and mischievous. Water is not passive scenery, but is imbued with energy, agency, humour and a life of its own, adapting according to the narrative. Likewise, with water in *Song of the Sea*: in the mischievous sea, Saoirse's brother Ben struggles despite the water being shallow enough to stand; the mystical sea enables Saoirse's encounter with the seals; the tumultuous sea drives Saoirse and her family into a storm; and the playful sea allows the siblings to swim happily.

Case study

In the classroom, the intention is for teachers to consider how posthumanism can offer children insight into these films. This invitation to posthumanism may be achieved by using arts-based methods and selected scenes from each film. *Song of the Sea* and *Ponyo* invite audiences to dive into the dreamlike world of the imagination: through movement, sound and image, these films capture the artistic affordances of the animation medium. Both films are therefore an effective stimulus for children's arts-based responses. The arts are wide-ranging: the below approaches focus on opportunities to draw, paint, collage and write poetry. First, it is useful to identify suggested film sequences that generate intrigue about humans and the sea (Table 12.1).

Table 12.1   Suggested film sequences

Ponyo	Song of the Sea
• The opening scenes of *Ponyo* • Ponyo is dragged along the seabed among debris and pollution • Ponyo rides the waves in search of Sōsuke	• Saorise and Ben on the beach near the start of the film • Saoirse discovers the selkie coat, wearing it to interact and swim with her fellow seals • The family are caught in the stormy seas

Suggested approaches for the above film sequences include the following:

• Children warm up for drawing and painting, by using a pencil to 'take a line for a walk' across a blank page, in response while listening to the soundtrack. Draw or paint underwater creatures they see and imagine, tuning into the imagery and the soundtrack.

• In role as the main characters, children move in response to the soundtrack, combining dance and drama. In keeping with posthumanism, this approach invites 'as if' behaviours (Daniel, 2021) through which children explore other ways to be. What can they see? What can they hear? How do they feel, both physically and emotionally? What is their connection with the sea?

• Choose art materials to depict the chosen sequence. For example, to represent Ponyo's encounter with the fishing trawler, create a collage by using waste materials, painting the sea and drawing Ponyo as a paper cut-out: this could be turned into a stop-motion animation using a simple app such as Stop Motion Studio.

• Discuss the significance of colour, camera, character, story, setting sound (3Cs and 3Ss); draw from questions from the 'Into Film 3Cs and 3Ss dice' (see resources) to develop discussion about animation.

• Provide still images from these sequences for children to discuss and annotate with descriptive words and phrases. Focus on the appearance and atmosphere of the sea at these points in the film.

• Eve Beane and Helen Wolstencroft explain that 'Poetry is the perfect multimodal text as it sings and dances off the page' (2007: 141). They suggest taking a visual approach to writing poetry, by looking closely at any atmospheric film sequence. With this in mind, the suggested scenes for both films offer visual and auditory stimulus ideal for children to write poetry. Children may begin by sharing vocabulary and phrases to describe the sea and the sea creatures (appearance, movement, sounds, how they might feel emotionally). Build on children's existing vocabulary by introduce new words. Children can choose which poetic form to write in as they reshape their responses into a poem.

CHAPTER SUMMARY

As this chapter has shown, despite its conceptual complexities, posthumanism can generate fascination and curiosity about the natural world and our place within it. A posthuman perspective enables us to reflect on diversity as we re-evaluate our interconnections with animals and environments in the context of a world shared with others. The value of biodiversity lies in its existence, and though we may never have direct experience of being in the ocean alongside a myriad of sea creatures, our interconnection with nonhuman animals and diverse ecosystems runs deep. Post-humanism and animated films for children make an effective pairing, and introducing *Song of the Sea* and *Ponyo* into primary school classrooms can provide valuable context for engagement with posthuman themes. For children unable to visit coastal environments, these animations can spark intrigue in the ocean; conversely, children who have been to the sea bring their experience to these films. Despite the environmental devastation caused by human impact upon the planet, it is encouraging that rewilding and rebuilding connection with nature are gaining momentum. This is seen in coral reef restoration projects, such as Hope Reef located off the coast of Sulawesi in Indonesia, which starts in the year 2019, when local island communities helped place onto the seabed restorative steel structures called Reef Stars, aptly arranged to spell the word HOPE. In the United Kingdom, David Attenborough's affecting, inspiring and influential *Blue Planet* series has drawn public attention to the issue of plastics in the world's oceans (Dunn et al., 2020). Documentary footage from Hope Reef and *Blue Planet II* can certainly invite children and adults alike to question the privileged status of the human, and emphasise our interdependence with the natural world. Nonetheless, the fictional realm of animated film can offer children a uniquely imagined posthuman perspective: *Ponyo* and *Song of the Sea* have the potential to engage children's interest in real-life encounters with nonhuman animals and environments, igniting a desire to celebrate biodiversity and guiding children toward a deeper understanding of their place within a diverse world.

REFLECTION

Note any other animated films that present posthuman themes, or refer to those mentioned in the earlier introduction to posthumanism. How could these animations be used to explore post-humanism with children? What characters would you focus on? What questions might you ask?

Note the titles of any children's fiction (picturebooks or novels) which depict the relationship between humans and nature, and in particular the sea.

From these children's books, what discussion points could arise in relation to posthuman ideas?

How might you invite children to respond to these ideas through arts-based approaches?

Further reading

Barton, M., Doherty, O., Jeffs, K., Ridgeon, W., Ruthven, J. and Smith, J. (Producers) (2017) *Blue Planet II*, Presented by David Attenborough. UK: BBC Natural History Unit. [documentary]

BFI Education (2003) *Look Again! A Teaching Guide for Using Film and Television With Three- to Eleven-Year Olds*. London: BFI Education.

Carrington, D. (12 March 2018) What is biodiversity and why does it matter to us? *The Guardian*. Available at: **https://www.theguardian.com/news/2018/mar/12/what-is-biodiversity-and-why-does-it-matter-to-us**

Hope Reef. Available at: **https://www.shebahopegrows.com/uk/home**.

Into Film 3Cs and 3Ss dice. Available at: **https://www.intofilm.org/resources/1282**.

National Geographic. Biodiversity. National Geographic Resource Library – Encyclopedic Entry. Available at: **https://www.nationalgeographic.org/encyclopedia/biodiversity/**.

United Nations: Sustainable Development Goals – Life Below Water. Available at: **https://www.un.org/sustainabledevelopment/oceans/**.

Primary texts

Coulais, B. (2014) *Song of the Sea Soundtrack*. Surrey: Wrasse Records. [audio].

Hall, D. and Williams, C. (directors) (2014) *Big Hero 6*. Burbank, CA: Walt Disney Pictures. [film].

Hisaishi, J. (2008) *Ponyo on the Cliff by the Sea Soundtrack*. Nürnberg: Colosseum Music Entertainment. [audio].

Miyazaki, H. (director) (2008) *Ponyo*. Tokyo: Studio Ghibli. [film].

Moore, T. (director) (2014) *Song of the Sea*. Ireland: Cartoon Saloon. [film].

Rianda, M. (director) (2021) *The Mitchells vs. The Machines*. Culver City, CA: Colombia Pictures. [film].

Stanton, A. (director) (2008) *Wall-E*. Burbank, CA: Walt Disney Pictures. [film].

References

Alaimo, S. (2010) *Bodily Natures: Science, Environment, and the Material Self*. Bloomington, IN: Indiana University Press.

Badmington, N. (2004) Mapping posthumanism. *Environment and Planning A, 36*(8): 1341–1363.

Bearne, E. and Wolstencroft, H. (2007) *Visual Approaches to Teaching Writing: Multimodal Literacy*. London: SAGE, pp. 5–11.

Boyd, B. (2007) Tails within tales. In L. Simmons and P. Armstrong (eds), *Knowing Animals*. Leiden: Brill.

Daniel, A. (2021) Classroom drama: learning through as-if behaviour. In S. Ogier and S. Tutchell (eds), *Teaching the Arts in the Primary Curriculum*. London: SAGE, Learning Matters.

Dasgupta, P. (2021) *The Economics of Nature: The Dasgupta Review*. London: HM Treasury.

Dunn, M.E., Mills, M. and Veríssimo, D. (2020) Evaluating the impact of the documentary series Blue Planet II on viewers' plastic consumption behaviours. *Conservation Science and Practice. A Journal of the Society for Conservation Biology, 2*(10): e280: 1–10.

Evans, J. (2004) Children's voices: children talking, drawing and writing about their out-of-school interests. In *Literacy Moves On: Using Popular Culture, New Technologies and Critical Literacy in the Primary Classroom*. London: David Fulton Publishers.

Flanagan, V. (2017) Posthumanism: rethinking 'the human' in modern children's literature. In C. Beauvais and N. Nikolajeva (eds), *The Edinburgh Companion to Children's Literature*. Edinburgh. Edinburgh University Press.

Haraway, D. (2003) *The Companion Species Manifesto: Dogs, People and Significant Others*. Chicago, IL: Prickly Paradigm Press.

Hayles, N.K. (1999) *How We Became Posthuman: Virtual Bodies in Cybernetics, Literature, and Informatics*. Chicago, IL: Chicago University Press.

Jaques, Z. (2015) *Children's Literature and the Posthuman: Animal, Environment, Cyborg*. Oxon: Routledge.

Maessen, V. and Umé, S. (2015) *Art Book: Song of the Sea*. Ireland: Cartoon Saloon and The Seal Factory.

Maine, F. (2015) *Teaching Comprehension Through Reading and Responding to Film*. Leicester: UKLA.

Malone, K., Duhn, I. and Tesar, M. (2020) Greedy bags of childhood nature theories. In A. Cutter-Mackenzie-Knowles, K. Malone and E. Barratt Hacking (eds), *Research Handbook on Childhoodnature: Assemblages of Childhood and Nature Research*. Cham: Springer Nature Switzerland AG.

Marsh, J. and Millard, E. (2000) Film and television. In Evans, J. (ed), *Literacy and Popular Culture: Using Children's Culture in the Classroom*. London: SAGE.

McCallum, R. (1999) *Ideologies of Identity in Adolescent Fiction: The Dialogic Construction of Subjectivity*. London: Routledge.

Miyazaki, H. (2009) A small seaside town. In *The Art of Ponyo on the Cliff: A Film by Hayao Miyazaki*. San Francisco, CA: Viz Media.

Murris, K. (2015) Posthumanism, philosophy for children, and Anthony Browne's 'little beauty'. *Bookbird*, 53(2): 59–65.

Murris, K. (2016) *The Posthuman Child: Educational Transformation Through Philosophy With Picture-books*. London: Routledge.

Ozaki, Y.T. (1908) The story of Urashima Taro, the Fisher Lad. In *Japanese Fairy Tales*. New York, NY: E.P. Dutton.

Reid, M. (2015) English and film: connecting children to the World. *Studies in Culture and Education*, 22(2): 189–198.

Serafini, F. (2014) *Reading the Visual: An Introduction to Teaching Multimodal Literacy*. New York, NY: Teachers College Press.

Watts, R. (2007) Harnessing the power of film in the primary classroom. *Literacy*, 41: 102–109.

Westling, L. (2006) Literature, the environment, and the question of the posthuman. In C. Gersdorf and S. Mayer (eds), *Nature in Literary and Cultural Studies: Transatlantic Conversations on Ecocriticism*. New York, NY: Rodopi.

Whitley, D. (2016) Human animals – transformations devoutly to be Wished? *Society and Animals*, 24(2): 208–212.

Wolfe, C. (2010) *What Is Posthumanism?* Minneapolis, MN: University of Minneapolis Press.

13

DIVERSITY MATTERS: PERSPECTIVES FOR TEACHING IN DESIGN AND TECHNOLOGY, SCIENCE AND EQUITY FOCUSED COMPUTING

LYNDA CHINAKA, SUE MCKINNEY AND SUE MILES-PEARSON

KEYWORDS: COMPUTING; CRITICAL RACE THEORY; CULTURALLY RESPONSIVE AND RELEVANT; DESIGN AND TECHNOLOGY; DIVERSITY; EQUITY; INTERSECTIONALITY; ROLE MODELS; SCIENCE; SOCIAL JUSTICE; UNDERREPRESENTED COMMUNITIES

CHAPTER OBJECTIVES

The aims of this chapter are:

- To recognise and harness the interest that children and young people have in computing [KD1] and STEM technologies and utilise this in the classroom.

- To increase teacher and practitioner's understanding around the underrepresentation of minority backgrounds in computing and STEM fields.
- To provide opportunities for children to recognise and research the success of people from their own heritage within computing and STEM subjects.
- To encourage increased participation and confidence of children of minority backgrounds in computing and STEM fields.

CCF ITE links

1.6	High-quality teaching has a long-term positive effect on pupils' life chances, particularly for children from disadvantaged backgrounds.
3	A school's curriculum enables it to set out its vision for the knowledge, skills and values that its pupils will learn, within a coherent wider vision for successful learning.
5.2	Seeking to understand pupils' differences, including their different levels of prior knowledge and potential barriers to learning, is an essential part of teaching.
7.4	Teachers can influence pupils to experience resilience and beliefs about their ability to succeed, by ensuring all pupils have the opportunity.

Why STEM/STEAM?

The skills and knowledge of the STEM (Science, Technology, Engineering and Mathematics) subjects reinforce learning and enhances the individual's understanding of each subject making clear connections between them. This was developed with the idea that it would encourage more equal opportunities. STEM was introduced into the primary classroom in 2010, after the Department for Education and Skills mapped the STEM landscape in 2006 by the Royal Academy of Engineers (RAE) and the Lloyds register Foundation (RAE, 2016), after a decision was made to try to bridge the gender gap across the subjects, as females were not as prevalent in the individual STEM subjects. This was not quite the resounding success that the organisers had hoped for (Morgan et al., 2016). However, promoting equality was not a new idea, as UNESCO (United Nations Education, Scientific and Cultural Organisation), that has been established since 1945, was ensuring that where possible education provided an equal opportunity for all, worldwide. It is still campaigning for equal opportunities today and its next goal on Sustainable Development is set for 'Education 2030 Framework for Action' (UNESCO, 2017).

In 2018, there was some development to the STEM agenda, as it was thought that it wasn't quite reaching enough of the desired female audience, so it was decided to include the Arts, making it into STEAM.

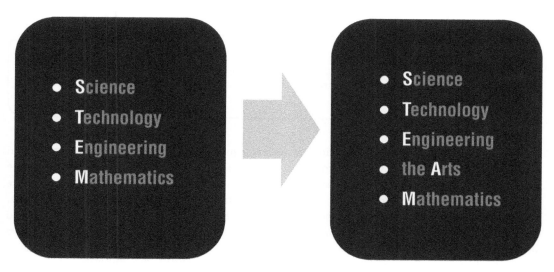

Figure 13.1   STEM becoming STEAM

STEM becoming STEAM was described by the Institute of Imagination as 'The glue between the elements … bridging the gap between imagination and learning' (Burry, 2018; Institution of Imagination, 2018). STEAM was officially launched in November 2019 at the 'National STEM into STEAM Day' (Milgrom-Elcott, 2019). STEAM education can provide children with flexibility, critical thinking, creativity, communication, transferable skills and collaboration.

D&T: disabilities, mental health and well-being, challenging stereotypes

D&T and primary education

Before we investigate how to challenge stereotypes and disabilities, we want to explain more about what design and technology (D&T) looks like in the primary classroom, and why it is such a vital element of the National Curriculum (2013). Pupils need to have the time to investigate and explore the world and products around them; being able to take risks in a safe environment. The design element is important, and the pupils do not have to be especially good at art, nevertheless it is important that they learn how to label their drawings accurately – with the relevant detail on the diagram, such as materials used and measurements. We should not lose sight of how making and creating something is very good for the child's mental health and designerly well-being (Stables, 2012), giving children the opportunity to have a sense of pride and satisfaction about what they have made, we will mention opportunities for STEM and STEAM initiatives which will allow more avenues for this well-being to manifest in the creative opportunities it provides.

REFLECTION

Think about people's experiences in lockdown during the COVID-19 pandemic. Why do you think people took up baking, gardening and craft projects? Was it because they had time or was it related also to well-being and mental health?

Before the pupils embark on making a final product it is important that they get the opportunity to make a prototype, to test out their design and consider if it is fit for intended purpose and meets the criteria. This part of the chapter will address several topics: the issue of gender stereotypes that are unconsciously embedded within D&T and how females in this field have always been fighting against male gender domination, and this is evident even today (Bystydzienski and Bird, 2006). It will also endeavour to address some of the speculation as to the expectations in D&T of children who have SEND, and that these children can achieve in the face of diversity. It will also look at the benefits of having D&T as part of the STEM curriculum, which has more recently become STEAM when the importance of including the Arts was recognised.

D&T is a subject that all children can access at their own level of ability, including children with English as an Additional Language (EAL) or who may have a Special Education Need or Disability (SEND). As stated in the SEN Code of Practice '...teachers should set high expectations for every pupil, whatever their prior attainment' (SEN COP, 2015). As D&T is a very practical subject, there is a lot of visual content and as thus is a universal language. It is also a subject in which the children are encouraged to investigate, explore and take 'safe' risks (Primary National Curriculum, 2013). Which is unlike a lot of other subjects where there is a definitive answer, and the children are often afraid to be wrong.

D&T is a relatively new subject that was introduced after the 1988 Education Reform Act (**http: www.legislation.gov.uk** 1988) (Waldon, 1993), which led to a revised National Curriculum 1993. It was launched initially into secondary schools and replaced many creative subjects including CDT (Craft, D&T). Before this change in the curriculum, I struggled in my own secondary schooling when I wanted to choose technical drawing as an option; teachers discouraged me from taking this subject, saying 'it was a boys' subject'. It was a struggle, but I succeeded being the only female in the group; however, this did not stop me from showing that I was an equal to my male peers.

REFLECTION

Think about when you had been in a situation where you felt you were not able to take the course that you wanted. What shaped that decision? Do you think the same views continue today? Are some subjects still seen as more appropriate for males or females?

D&T within the National Curriculum has evolved, and after 1993, significant changes including the introduction of a specific curriculum subject for D&T in the primary school for Key Stages 1 and 2.

This had the potential to change the way that primary schools teach (Waldon, 1993). In the late 1990s, the qualification curriculum authority (QCA) produced schemes of work for the wider curriculum subjects (QCA, 1998). These were designed to benefit the teachers as they had the key elements needed to plan a project reflecting on the national curriculum. However, they were mainly a skeleton of expectations, such as hand/eye coordination and fine motor skills, which teachers had to add flesh out to make it more interesting. Teachers should not lose sight of the benefits that accompany a D&T lesson for children with SEND, for instance the application of discussion about the design of a product and the importance of reflection and manipulation to improve their designs.

In 2013, the most recent edition of the primary National Curriculum was introduced; this publication had gone from being quite prescriptive to extremely open, allowing the teachers to use the breadth of both core and wider curriculum subjects to enhance and allow creativity in the ways that they taught the subject, ensuring it was inclusive for all (NC, 2013).

Case study: primary class teacher

A case study from a past D&T specialist, who has been working in a primary school for several years, has had the opportunity to explore how the children in the class got on with a project of making puppets. There were a significant number of children with EAL within the class, and many of them struggled with English and mathematics, which incorporated a lot more reading and writing to successfully complete the work.

The class teacher found that although some reading and some writing was involved with the annotating of the design, writing the method and resource list, the children managed the expectations and were more enthusiastic about getting on and finishing their work.

The following photographs are from this case study (Figures 13.2 and 13.3).

You can see a good example of the fine motor skills that the children need to assemble their puppets (Figure 13.4).

Figure 13.2   Beginning to assemble a puppet

Figure 13.3   In this photograph you can see that the child has designed her puppet and made a list of the resources needed and the method

Figure 13.4   Finished product

It is also very important to get children to evaluate their finished product against their initial design. Does it meet the criteria and is it fit for purpose and what would they do differently if they made it again.

The class teacher also found that she did not have to adapt her lesson as much as for other subjects, as they all coped quite well with the task and seemed to enjoy themselves and met the learning objective.

This case study speaks volumes about the diversity of D&T, and no matter how many challenges that children might have with their learning, the process of designing, making and evaluating within D&T can help the children overcome obstacles such as a lack of self-esteem, confidence in communicating and expressing their views and ideas with others, as well as the breadth of cultural knowledge and understanding that children can bring to the class from their own backgrounds, such as different techniques and approaches to do a task (Miles-Pearson, 2020).

Therefore, I think that combining D&T as part of a cross-curricular project could be very rewarding for the children and the teacher.

Science: black lives matter/race/critical race theory

This section is about challenging the diversity and stereotypes of the choices of scientists within the National Curriculum. It will be an introduction to a variety of ethnically diverse scientists and their successes that not only reflect the children's own cultural capital but will also introduce children to successful people from their own ethnic cultures that are not reflected in the National Curriculum at the moment!

In a brief introduction to the Critical Race Theory and the 'intersectionality', Professor Kimberley Cranshaw, University of California, has identified an excluded population of African American women who fall between her 'frames'. The TED Talks 'intersectionality' outlines the double discrimination that black African American women are faced with. Cranshaw describes two frames in terms of job opportunities: African American (as being identified as male) and women (as being white). An employer can therefore tick boxes when employing either a African American male or a women. The African American women, however, fall between these two frames, which is, as Kimberle Cranshaw terms, 'intersectionality'. She calls for a third frame which just incorporates Black African women and includes both their gender and race. Her term for the existing 2 frames is 'injustice squared'. Professor Cranshaw also founded the hashtag #sayhername to remember all the unknown or unreported Black African American women who have died at the hands of the police.

REFLECTION

How many female scientists or engineers can you name? How many Black or Asian female scientists can you name? While there are now quite a few female celebrity historians on television, how many female presenters of scientific programmes can you think of?

Why does this matter in the classroom? Perhaps taking #sayhername further, it was only when George Floyd – an African American man – was killed by the police that this reached the headlines and consequently the *Black Lives Matter* became a global movement. Since his death, by the Minneapolis police officer Derek Chauvin (who was eventually charged with second-degree murder), the social movement *Black Lives Matter* has become more prominent as a political force to open people's eyes to racism. One of the offshoots from this movement is the need to better educate people to recognise fascism in all its forms and where better to start than in Primary School!

While these examples relate to African American experiences, it is true to say that similar attitudes exist in Britain. Within academia only 0.7% identify as Black and 7.0% as Asian (Gewin, 2020). Recognition of the problem has led to the creation of BBSTEM (Black British STEM), a support and mentoring group to promote increased representation (**https://bbstem.co.uk/**).

Another consequence from this movement was the 'taking the knee' at prominent sports events which was occasionally booed by the spectators. The 'taking the knee' is viewed as being a protest, whereas not taking the knee was more viewed as a need to educate. In this section we are therefore not taking the knee and thinking about education. We are raising awareness, and the purpose is to educate children which gives them the choice to bring about change in the future.

Scientists that could be included to represent the diversity of the classroom could be:

- Donald Palmer

- Jassel Majevadia

- Maggie Aderin-Pocock

- Saiful Islam

- Charlotte Armah

- Harry Bhadeshia

- Mah Hussain-Gambles

- Mark Richards

- Sanfeev Gupta

- Hope Mwanake

- Ashitey Trebi-Ollennu

(STEM.org)

Between 1966 and 1977, the social scientist David Chambers asked 4,807 children, mostly from Canada and the United States, to draw a scientist. From their illustrations it was apparent that they believed scientists wore white coats, eyeglasses, lab equipment and carried books and were mostly white-haired men (Chambers, 1983). They found that when the children were asked to draw a scientist, the results revealed a stunning bias: 99.4% of the drawings depicted a male scientist. Out of 5,000 drawings collected between 1966 and 1977, only 28 were of female scientists, all of which were drawn by girls.

This piece of research (DAST) is largely also relevant to today's children's understanding of what a scientist is. It could be said that children cannot therefore empathise with these because they are 'not like me'(Zhai et al., 2014). The aim here is to break down the pre-conceptions that science is not for 'them' and show scientists from diverse backgrounds, cultures and gender to encourage children to identify with successful scientists and perhaps offer the proposal that they too could become successful scientists. The social media representation of scientists is also no help as it usually portrays not only white-haired men but crazy white-haired men.

Women scientists have started to rage against the typical stereotypes and as the following article suggests have begun to smash through the glass ceilings (**https://www.bbc.co.uk/news/science-environment-48953793**).

Likewise young scientists have begun to make themselves known as illustrated by this article on scientists who take selfies: **https://www.americanscientist.org/blog/macroscope/scientists-who-selfie-break-down-stereotypes**.

Case study

This research was important to me as, as a woman from an Indian background, I found myself wondering why I never saw myself represented at school. To be honest, I do not remember learning about a single female scientist, let alone one of colour. Times have changed and the world is becoming more diverse and multicultural; schools need to reflect this so more children can see themselves in the figures they learn about and feel inspired to achieve their best and more.

This comment by a final year student's dissertation led to a project to design a creative activity based around the women of the space industry of the past. The aim was to combat the concept of inter-sectionality by presenting children with positive female scientists and engineers (Sinclair and Strachen, 2018). It was important initially to research carefully to discover role models. Once begun, however, it was obvious that this was a rich area for development. The project effectively linked history and science including historical research and practical science activities.

Children could look at:

- The effect of meteors and meteorites while investigating the work of Ursula Mavin.

- Wind turbines and engineering with Mary Jackson

- Planning, preparing and monitoring the food for Apollo 11 astronauts in quarantine with Jackie Stewart

- Computation and calculation with Dorothy Vaughn and Katherine Johnson

- Astronauts in space with Mae Jemison

An extension of the project would be to consider what the role of women is now and how they are involved with future space exploration. Contacting female scientists directly to ask about their work would broaden children's perspectives.

This website highlights the importance of women to the NASA programmes (**https://www.nasa. gov/stem/womenstem/women-in-space.html**).

Computing: diversity and equity in computing

This segment of the chapter is intended to increase teachers' awareness and understanding of equity in relation to children from underrepresented backgrounds, specifically Black children and the way that experiences of curriculum affect outcomes and ultimately attainment. The subject focus is computing.

The increasing prevalence of computing technologies in our lives continues at pace following national lockdowns during the COVID-19 pandemic. Computing's ubiquitous nature sees adults and children alike rely upon the extraordinary impact that it makes upon everyday life. Children and young people have grown up with computing and value the life skills they are able to build. However, the Royal Society report (2017) found that interest 'in computing in schools continues to dwindle' in spite of curriculum changes (Royal Society, 2017).

This issue is further compounded by the fact that interest in computing for children from underrepresented communities, specifically Black children, appears to decrease as children progress through the education hierarchy in the United Kingdom. Research conducted by Kemp and others report that the number of students pursuing computing qualifications at GSE and Advanced level is disappointing with 'fewer females, pupils from working class and in particular fewer minority ethnic students' (Kemp et al., 2018).

There are several factors that contribute to this. One of these is the number of societal cues that help to perpetuate a 'this isn't for me feeling' among Black pupils when they do not see themselves represented on TV, in schools, online, in employment in these computing occupations. When they do not see themselves represented in the field or wider society as programmers, computer scientists or engineers, they may be discouraged and lack the self-belief that would lead them into STEM or STEAM based careers. The individuals they do see in these places are often white. Authors researching the take up of computing in schools assert the idea that high standards of excellence that are often associated with computing and who does it might further alienate Black students, making them removed 'from that of the idealised computer science student' (Copsey-Blake et al., 2021). The lack of self-belief or the capacity for Black pupils to see themselves as experts in the field of computing is not uncommon. The Hamilton Commission report (2021) illuminates some of the negative experiences of Black students in the education system that in turn had the effect of discouraging students from obtaining qualifications in STEM subjects; Sir Lewis Hamilton provides insights about this linked to his own experiences of the education system. Through the report, recommendations call for change in the curriculum. Inspiring outreach activities that centres in Black community organisations are suggested to stimulate and accelerate the progress that can be made in school.

Calls for more equitable learning in schools to enrich the experiences of children from underrepresented communities in computing has gathered momentum following the death of George Floyd in 2020 in the United States. Teaching topics that reflect the heritage, perspectives and life experiences is likely to stimulate their interest and engage them. Starting points that include the study of culture is effective in the classroom. This must go beyond the surface of producing attractive displays and artefacts that are indicative of students from these communities. Rather, it should also 'offer an emotionally stable and responsive environment' that inspires harmony and promotes genuine trust in pupils (Hammond, 2014).

Computing can be used in this context to deliver topics that are of interest to students but are underpinned by robust objectives. Computing topics can be formulated and planned in relation to the interests of the local school population. This is exemplified in the publication 'Culturally relevant and responsive computing in the classroom: A guide for curriculum design and teaching' (Leonard et al., 2021).

Case study

The following case study centres around a group of PGCE Primary Education ITE students who have just returned from an initial seven-week placement in school. Students created computational artefacts inspired by a discussion on culture.

An initial activity was devised to promote conversation amongst peers in the classroom. They are asked to consider the word 'culture' and what it represents to them. Working collaboratively, they record their responses. Initial reactions were linked to dress, food, religion and customs. When students explored the theme further, they began to share insights on a deeper level with each other. On discussing observances at a Somali wedding, one student revealed she had never shared information like this in a formal setting. Black students enjoyed an exchange about cultural cues that shaped them, and the nuances of particular words spoken at different times of the day. Another student explained the significance of a church service and ritual that her family participates in on annual trips to their ancestral home in Italy.

The interaction between students was remarkable. Students engage in conversations around topics that would not ordinarily be discussed in an institutional setting. Allowing students to talk freely with each other in a formal setting also helps in developing agency. This was distinct from the norm type of talk in the classroom that usually takes place. Discourse in the classroom is often dominated by the teacher. A teacher–pupil mode is often in place with the teacher dominating with teacher talk and pupils passively receiving in an orderly fashion. This is contrary 'to the way that students who are culturally and linguistically diverse, engage in discourse outside school and at home' (Hammond, 2014) (Figures 13.5 and 13.6).

When students see that their experiences and perspectives are valued during learning, they become more engaged. It becomes the responsibility of the teacher to build awareness and strengthen their own awareness of their students' perspectives and cultural dispositions. Increasing their own understanding of societal factors that might affect their students is equally as important. The capacity to do so will impact on the ability to use the learning gained to plan robust and relevant computing objectives that match some of the topics and areas of interest to students. Computing curricula can be devised to support the teaching of current topics including climate change and social justice. Enduring and contemporary issues that particularly affect Black people such as algorithmic bias and facial recognition can be taught through computing.

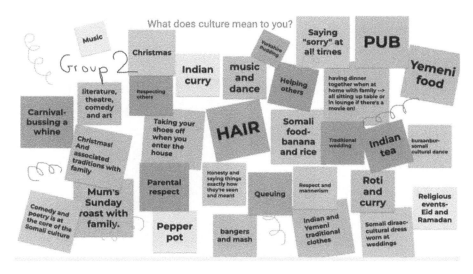

Figure 13.5   PGCE ITE students share ideas about culture and what it means to them

Figure 13.6   PGCE ITE students consider how the term 'culture' may be interpreted

A strategy that advocates a 'justice oriented approach to computer science education' (Madkins and Howard, 2021) encourages students to use their own learning to define success for themselves. Offering opportunities to work in Google or Microsoft may not necessarily be of interest to students from underrepresented backgrounds. Rather, supporting them in their efforts to use skills and knowledge in computing for pursuits that are meaningful to them and or their community is key. The parameters for success may need to be redefined to accommodate alternative aspirations and viewpoints. Making learning equitable would include a response that incorporates response from teachers that is expansive and admits student perspectives and experiences when curriculums are devised. An equitable example of this is evidenced in the new 'Culturally relevant and responsive computing in the classroom: A guide for curriculum design and teaching' (Leonard et al., 2021) (Figure 13.7).

Figure 13.7   Students produced a computational artefact with content drawn from work completed in a photo editor as well as a video. Theme is based on women of colour in tech

---

REFLECTION

What sort of projects could we do with children in school that would help them identify how they could use computing to support or benefit their communities?

CHAPTER SUMMARY

From this chapter, looking at diversity in the primary classroom, we hope that teachers will have a greater understanding of how they can reflect on the intent of the lesson and adapt their teaching so that this can be implemented through the lenses of Science, Computing and D&T.

Podcasts and videos

TED Talk: Reshma Saujani 'Teach girls bravery, not perfection' **https://www.youtube.com/watch?v=fC9da6eqaqg**.

Designed for Life Podcasts (Design and Technology Association and The Edge Foundation).

Tony Ryan interviews:

- Tori Stewart, describes himself as a 'multi-disciplined creative chameleon', working with big brands. **https://podcasts.apple.com/gb/podcast/designed-for-life/id1528885120?i=1000519277047**

- Zoe Laughlin, British artist, maker and self-confessed tinkerer and materials engineer: **https://podcasts.apple.com/gb/podcast/designed-for-life/id1528885120?i=1000508578426**

- Jaamar Semper, MasterChef semi finalist: **https://podcasts.apple.com/gb/podcast/designed-for-life/id1528885120?i=1000521968057**

- Ella Podmore, IET – Young Woman Engineer of the year 2021: **https://podcasts.apple.com/gb/podcast/designed-for-life/id1528885120?i=1000523256593**

References

Burry, M. (2018) *Why Was Art Added to Science, Technology, Engineering and Maths education?* Available at: **https://www.nymetroparents.com/article/how-stem-became-steam**

Bystydzienski, J. and Bird, R. (2006) *Women in Academic Science, Technology, Engineering and Mathematics.* Recovering Barriers. Bloomington, IN: Indiana University Press.

Chambers, D.W. (1983) Stereotypic images of the scientist: the draw a scientist test. *Science Education*, *67*(2): 255–265. **https://doi.org/10.1002/sce.3730670213**.

Copsey Blake, M., Hamer, J., Kemp, P.E.J. and Wong, B. (2021) *Should We Be Concerned About Who is Studying Computing in Schools?* Cambridge: Raspberry Pi Foundation.

DfE (2013) *National Curriculum for Design & Technology Programme of Study: Key Stages 1 & 2*. Available at: **https://assets.publishing.service.gov.uk/government/uploads/system/uploads/attachment_data/file/239041/PRIMARY_national_curriculum_-_Design_and_technology.pdf** (accessed 21 April 2022)

DfE (2015) *Special Education Needs and Disability Code of Practice 0-25*. Available at: **https://assets.publishing.service.gov.uk/government/uploads/system/uploads/attachment_data/file/398815/SEND_Code_of_Practice_January_2015.pdf** (accessed 21 April 2022)

Education Reform Act (1988) c2. Available at: **https://www.legislation.gov.uk/ukpga/1988/40/contents** (accessed 18 April 2022)

Gewin, V. (2020) 'Blood, sweat and tears': building a network for Black scientists. *Nature*. Available at: **https://www.nature.com/articles/d41586-020-03279-0**

Hammond, Z. (2014) *Culturally Responsive Teaching and the Brain*. London: SAGE Publications Ltd CA.

Institute of Imagination (2018) Available at: **https://ioi.london/imagination-lab/**

Kemp, P.E.J., Berry, M.G. and Wong, B. (2018) *The Roehampton Annual Computing Education Report: Data from 2017*. London: University of Roehampton.

Leonard, H.A., Sentence, S., Kirby, D., Chinaka, L., Deutsch, M., Dimitriadi, Y. and Goode, J. (2021) *Localising Culturally Responsive Computing Teaching to an English Context: Developing Teacher Guidelines*. Cambridge: Raspberry Pi Foundation

Madkins, T. and Howard, N.R. (2021) *Equity-Focused Teaching in K-12 CS: Strategies for Teachers, Teacher Educators, and Districts*. Available at: **https://www.researchgate.net/publication/357240602_Equity-focused_teaching_in_K-12_CS_strategies_for_teachers_teacher_educators_and_districts** (accessed 21 April 2022)

Miles-Pearson, S. (2020) Chapter 2, exploring food education in the primary school curriculum. In M. Rutland and A. Turner (eds), *Food Education and Food Technology in School Curricula International Perspectives*. Switzerland: Springer Publication.

Milgrom-Elcott, T. (7 November 2019) When STEM becomes STEAM we can change the game. *Forbes*. Available at: https://www.forbes.com/sites/taliamilgromelcott/2019/11/07/when-stem-becomes-steam-we-can-change-the-game/?sh=5b9f8ff76905

Morgan, Kirby and Stamenkovic (2016) *The UK STEM Education Landscape*. Available at: **https://www.raeng.org.uk/publications/reports/uk-stem-education-landscape** (accessed 21 April 2022)

Qualification and Curriculum Authority (1998) *Qualification and Curriculum Authority*. Available at: https://www.qca.org.uk/index.html (accessed 21 April 2022)

SEN Code of Practice (2015) Available at: **https://councilfordisabledchildren.org.uk/resources/all-resources/filter/education-and-learning/education-support-children-and-young-people**

Sinclair, A. and Strachan, A. (2018) Standing on the shoulders of giants: contemporary scientists bringing your science curriculum to life. *Primary Science*, *151*: 10. Association for Science Education. STEM.org website. Available at: **https://www.stem.org.uk/resources/collection/4372/inspiring-scientists?page=1**

Stables, K. (2012) Designerly well-being: can mainstream schooling offer a curriculum that provides a foundation for developing the lifelong design and technological capability of individuals and societies? *Technology Education in 21st Century PATT26 Conference.* Available at: https://www.academia.edu/8888157/Designerly_well_being_Can_mainstream_schooling_offer_a_curriculum_that_provides_a_foundation_for_developing_the_lifelong_design_and_technological_capability_of_individuals_and_societies (accessed 21 April 2022)

The Hamilton Commission (2021) *Accelerating Change: Improving Representation of Black People in UK Motorsport.* London: The Royal Academy of Engineering.

The Royal Society (2017) *After the Reboot: Computing Education in UK Schools.* London: The Royal Society.

UNESCO (2017) *Education 2030 Framework for Action.* Available at: **http://uis.unesco.org/sites/default/files/documents/education-2030-incheon-framework-for-action-implementation-of-sdg4-2016-en_2.pdf**

Waldon, A. (1993) Chapter 9, some equality issues in primary design and technology. In H. Claire, J. Maybin and J. Swan (eds), *Equality Matters: A Case Study From the Primary School.* Clevedon: Multilingual Matters Ltd.

Zhai, J., Jocz, J.A. and Tan, A.-L. (2014) 'Am I like a scientist?': primary children's images of doing science in school. *International Journal of Science Education, 36*(4).

INDEX